pocket guide to

RIFLES

identification and values

1900 to present

Russell Quertermous

Steve Quertermous

cb

COLLECTOR BOOKS

A Division of Schroeder Publishing Co., Inc.

The current values in this book should be used only as guide. They are not intended to set prices, which vary from one section of the country to another. Auction prices as well as dealer prices vary greatly and are affected by condition as well as demand. Neither the Author nor the Publisher assumes responsibility for any losses that might be incurred as a result of consulting this guide.

Seaching for a Publisher?
We are always looking for knowledgeable people considered experts within their fields. If you feel there is a real need for a book on your collectible subject and have a large comprehensive collection, contact us.

COLLECTOR BOOKS
P.O. Box 3009
Paducah, Kentucky 42002-3009

Introduction

This is an identification and value guide. Very little in the way of instruction and directions should be required to use a value guide but some words of explanation might be in order.

First of all the suggested values are just that. They are not the final word on an item's absolute worth. That figure can only be determined by the buyer's willingness to purchase and the seller's ability to hold to an asking price. But the values found in this book should be a reasonable guide of what certain firearms are selling for on average around the country.

Geography plays an important part in establishing value. Some guns are more in demand in particular locales than other firearms that are equal in rarity, workmanship and quantities. There are also guns that have a good resale value just because they are manufactured by a particular company. Maybe the company's track record for producing high quality firearms is especially good. Or, maybe there is just an aura of greatness that has been associated with the manufacturer for one reason or another.

Condition is also important in establishing a value. The values in this guide relate to firearms in very good to excellent condidion. That is: in good working condition with no appreciable wear on working surfaces, no corrosion or pitting with only minor surface dents or scratches at one end of the spectrum to: in new condition, used very little, with no noticeable marring of the wood or metal and with perfect bluing except at the muzzle or on sharp edges.

The value range should be a reasonable guide to the gun's real selling worth. But readers who disagree with the pricing structure are encouraged to do further research to ascertain what they consider to be the value.

The illustrations in this guide are from gun companies' promotional materials and as such are not meant to be representative of size relation.

There is no way that a book of this size can be all inclusive of the firearms made in the world but we hope it is a good survey of most of the firearms that are readily available on the open market.

Acknowledgments

The companies included for the use of catalogs, advertisements and promotional material.

A special thanks to the following gun manufacturers for additional photos, information and assistance: Browning, Charter Arms Corp., Colt Industries, Firearms Division, Harrington & Richardson, Inc., Heckler & Koch, Interarms for material on Mark X rifles, Ithaca Gun Co., Kleinguenther, Inc., Mannlicher, Marlin for material on Marlin and Marlin-Glenfield, O.F. Mossberg & Sons, Inc. for material on Mossberg and New Haven, Remington, Savage Arms for material on Savage rifles, Stevens rifles, and Anschutz rifles, Universal Firearms, Weatherby, Inc., Winchester-Western for material on Winchester rifles, and U.S. Repeating Arms for material on Winchester rifles.

Petersen Publishing Company for the use of photographs from *Guns and Ammo Annual*, 1977, 1982 and *Hunting Annual* 1983.

Stackpole Books for the use of photographs from W.H.B. Smith's *Book of Rifles.*

Russell Scheffer of Scheffer Studio for graphic arrangement of the material. Russell is always there, day or night, to crank out an amazing amount of work on extremely short notice.

The crew that makes up the editorial staff of Collector Books. Their dedication and hard work make an unbelievable number of books on antiques and collectibles indispensible tools for collectors everywhere.

Contents

Anschutz

Anschutz Model 64

Anschutz Model 64S

Anschutz Model 1407, 1807, 1407L, & 1807L
Caliber: 22 long rifle
Action: Bolt action; 1407L & 1807L left hand action (add $50.00)
Magazine: None; single shot
Barrel: Blued; 26"
Stock & Forearm: Walnut one-piece pistol grip stock & wide forearm; thumb rest; cheekpiece; adjustable butt plate
Estimated Value: $480.00 - $600.00

Anschutz Model 184
Caliber: 22 long rifle
Action: Bolt action; repeating
Magazine: 5-shot detachable clip
Barrel: Blued; 21½"
Stock & Forearm: Checkered walnut Monte Carlo one-piece pistol grip stock & lipped forearm; swivels
Estimated Value: $200.00 - $250.00

Anschutz Model 64 & 64L Match
Caliber: 22 long rifle
Action: Bolt action; 64L left hand action (add $20.00)
Magazine: None; single shot
Barrel: Blued; 26"
Stock & Forearm: Match style; checkered walnut one-piece pistol grip stock & forearm; thumb rest; cheekpiece; adjustable butt plate
Estimated Value: $280.00 - $350.00

Anschutz Model 64S & 64SL Match
Similar to the Model 64 & 64L except: special match sights; add $20.00 for left hand version (64SL)
Estimated Value: $300.00 - $375.00

Anschutz Mark 12 Target
Similar to the Model 64 except: heavier barrel; non-adjustable butt plate; handstop; tapered stock & forearm
Estimated Value: $260.00 - $325.00

Anschutz Model 54

Anschutz Model 54M
Similar to Model 54 except: 22 Winchester magnum; 4-shot clip
Estimated Value: $285.00 - $360.00

Anschutz Model 54
Caliber: 22 long rifle
Action: Bolt action; repeating
Magazine: Detachable 5-shot clip or 10-shot clip
Barrel: Blued; 24"
Stock & Forearm: Checkered walnut Monte Carlo one-piece pistol grip stock & lipped forearm
Estimated Value: $260.00 - $325.00

Anschutz

Anschutz Model 153

**Anschutz Model 1432
& 1432D Custom**
Caliber: 22 Hornet
Action: Bolt action; repeating
Magazine: 5-shot clip
Barrel: Blued; 24"
Stock & Forearm: Checkered walnut
Monte Carlo one-piece pistol grip
stock & lipped forearm; swivels
Estimated Value: $500.00 - $625.00

**Anschutz Model 1422D, 1522D,
& 1532D, Custom**
Similar to the Model 1432D Custom
except: different calibers; 1422D is
22 long rifle; 1522D is 22 magnum;
1532D is 222 Remington
Estimated Value:

1422D	1522D	1532D
$560.00	$580.00	$520.00
$700.00	$725.00	$650.00

**Anschutz Model 1422DCL,
1522DCL, & 1532DCL, Classic**
Similar to the Custom models
except: without deluxe features.
Checkered walnut, one-piece pistol
grip stock & tapered forearm
Estimated Value:
1422DCL: $520.00 - $650.00
1522DCL: $530.00 - $670.00
1532DCL: $480.00 - $600.00

Anschutz Bavarian 1700, 1700D
Caliber: 22 long rifle, 22 magnum,
22 Hornet, or 222 Remington; add
10% for 22 magnum, 22 Hornet or
222 Remington
Action: Bolt action; adjustable
trigger
Magazine: 5-shot clip
Barrel: 24" blued
Stock & Forearm: Select checkered
Monte Carlo walnut one-piece pistol
grip stock & forearm; swivels
Estimated Value: $745.00 - $930.00

Anschutz Model 141
Caliber: 22 long rifle or 22 magnum
Action: Bolt action; repeating
Magazine: Detachable 5-shot clip
Barrel: Blued; 24"
Stock & Forearm: Checkered walnut
Monte Carlo one-piece pistol grip
stock & forearm
Estimated Value: $210.00 - $260.00

Anschutz Model 153
Similar to the Model 141 except:
abruptly ended forearm trimmed in
different wood
Estimated Value: $220.00 - $275.00

Anschutz Achiever
Caliber: 22 long rifle
Action: Bolt action; repeating
Magazine: 5 or 10-shot clip; single
shot adapter
Barrel: 18½" blued
Stock & Forearm: Stippled
European hardwood one-piece pistol
grip stock & forearm; vent louvers;
adjustable stock
Estimated Value: $235.00 - $295.00

Anschutz

Anschutz Model 64MS

Anschutz Model 1418

Anschutz Model 64MS
Caliber: 22 long rifle
Action: Bolt action; adjustable two-stage trigger
Magazine: None; single shot
Barrel: 21¼" medium heavy
Stock & Forearm: Silhouette-style one-piece stippled pistol grip stock & forearm
Estimated Value: $530.00 - $665.00

Anschutz Model 54.18MS
Similar to the Model 64MS except: 22" barrel; add 5% for left hand model; add 15% for Repeating Model; 35% for Repeating Deluxe
Estimated Value: $880.00 - $1,100.00

Anschutz Model 164
Caliber: 22 long rifle
Action: Bolt action; repeating
Magazine: 5-shot clip or 10-shot clip
Barrel: Blued; 23"
Stock & Forearm: Checkered walnut Monte Carlo one-piece pistol grip stock & lipped forearm
Estimated Value: $260.00 - $325.00

Anschutz Model 164M
Similar to the Model 164 except: 22 Winchester magnum; 4-shot clip
Estimated Value: $280.00 - $350.00

Anschutz Model 1418 & 1418D
Caliber: 22 long rifle
Action: Bolt action; repeating; double set or single set trigger
Magazine: 5-shot clip or 10-shot clip
Barrel: Blued; 19¾"
Stock & Forearm: Checkered European Monte Carlo stock & full-length forearm; cheekpiece; swivels
Estimated Value: $620.00 - $770.00

Anschutz Model 1518, 1518D
Similar to the Model 1418 except: in 22 WMR only 4-shot clip magazine. Currently called 1518D.
Estimated Value: $630.00 - $785.00

Anschutz Model 1416D & 1516D
Similar to the Model 1418D & 1518D except: regular length forearm; different stock with more defined pistol grip; 23" barrel; add $20.00 for 22 magnum (1516D)
Estimated Value: $405.00 - $510.00

Anschutz Model 1433D
Similar to the Model 1418D except: 22 Hornet caliber
Estimated Value: $560.00 - $700.00

Anschutz Model 1411 & 1811
Caliber: 22 long rifle
Action: Bolt action
Magazine: None; single shot
Barrel: 27½" heavy
Sights: None; tapped for scope
Stock & Forearm: Select walnut one-piece Monte Carlo pistol grip stock & forearm; adjustable cheekpiece; hand rest swivel; adjustable butt plate; a match-style rifle
Estimated Value: $550.00 - $625.00

Anschutz Model 520

Anschutz Mark 2000
Caliber: 22 long rifle
Action: Bolt action; hammerless
Magazine: None; single shot
Barrel: Blued; 26"; medium heavy
Stock & Forearm: Smooth hardwood one-piece semi-pistol grip stock & forearm; a match rifle designed for young shooters
Estimated Value: $160.00 - $200.00

Anschutz Model 520 Sporter or Mark525 Sporter
Caliber: 22 long rifle
Action: Semi-automatic
Magazine: 10-shot clip
Barrel: Blued; 24"
Stock & Forearm: Checkered walnut Monte Carlo semi-pistol stock & fluted forearm; presently called Mark 525 Sporter
Estimated Value: $310.00 - $390.00

Armalite

Armalite AR-180 Sporter

Armalite AR-7 Explorer

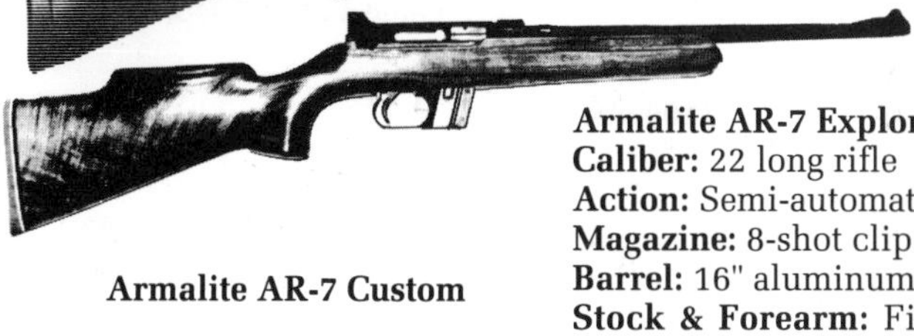

Armalite AR-7 Custom

Armalite AR-180 Sporter
Caliber: 223
Action: Semi-automatic, gas operated
Magazine: 5-shot detachable box
Barrel: Blued; 18"
Stock & Forearm: Pistol grip; nylon folding stock; fiberglass forearm
Estimated Value: $460.00 - $575.00

Armalite AR-7 Explorer
Caliber: 22 long rifle
Action: Semi-automatic
Magazine: 8-shot clip
Barrel: 16" aluminum; steel lined
Stock & Forearm: Fiberglass pistol grip stock (no forearm); stock used as case for gun when dismantled; after about 1973 marketed as Charter Arms AR-7
Estimated Value: $70.00 - $90.00

Armalite AR-7 Custom
A sport version of the AR-7 Explorer with a walnut Monte Carlo one-piece pistol grip stock & forearm; slightly heavier
Estimated Value: $85.00 - $110.00

Browning

Browning 78

Browning 78 Govt. 45-70

Browning 78 Round Barrel

Browning 78 Govt. 45-70
Similar to 78 except: Government 45-70 caliber with iron sights & straight grip stock, octagonal bull barrel
Estimated Value: $335.00 - $420.00

Browning 78
Caliber: 22-250, 6mm mag., 7mm mag., 25-06, or 30-06
Action: Falling block, lever action; exposed hammer
Magazine: None; single shot
Barrel: Blued; 26" round or octagon
Stock & Forearm: Checkered walnut Monte Carlo pistol grip stock & forearm; a replica of John Browning's first patented rifle in 1878
Estimated Value: $340.00 - $425.00

Browning T Bolt T-1

Browning T Bolt T-2

Browning T Bolt T-2
A fancy version of the T-Bolt T-1 with checkered stock & forearm
Estimated Value: $320.00 - $400.00

Browning T Bolt T-1
Caliber: 22 short, long, or long rifle
Action: Bolt action; hammerless; side ejection; repeating; single shot conversion
Magazine: Removable 5-shot box
Barrel: Blued; 22"
Stock & Forearm: Walnut one-piece pistol grip stock & forearm
Estimated Value: $260.00 - $325.00

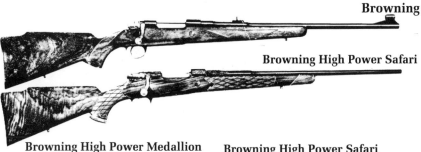

Browning High Power Safari

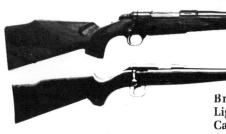

Browning High Power Medallion

Browning High Power Medallion
A higher grade version of the Safari with more engraving & higher quality wood
Estimated Value: $960.00 - $1,200.00

Browning High Power Olympian
Highest grade of High Power models with complete engraving & some gold inlay
Estimated Value: $1,600.00 - $2,000.00

Browning High Power Safari
Caliber: 243, 270, 30-06, 308, 300 mag., or 375 mag. (in 1960); later the following calbers were added: 264, 338, 222, 22-250, 243, and 7mm mag.
Action: Mauser-type bolt action; in long, medium, or short action; repeating
Magazine: 3 or 5-shot clip, depending on caliber
Barrel: Blued; 22" or 24"
Stock & Forearm: Checkered walnut Monte Carlo one-piece pistol grip stock & forearm; magnum calibers have recoil pad; swivels
Estimated Value: $640.00 - $800.00

Browning Model BBR

Browning Model 52 Ltd. Edition

Browning Model 52 Ltd. Edition
Caliber: 22 long rifle
Action: Bolt action; repeating; adjustable trigger
Magazine: 5-shot, detachable box
Barrel: 24"
Stock & Forearm: Checkered high-grade walnut, pistol grip one-piece stock and forearm; rosewood fore-end
Estimated Value: $300.00 - $375.00

Browning Model BBR & BBR Lightning Bolt
Caliber: 30-06 Sprg., 270 Win., 25-06 Rem., 7mm Rem. mag., or 300 Win. mag.
Action: Bolt action; short throw; cocking indicator; repeating
Magazine: 4-shot; 3-shot in magnum; hinged floorplate, detachable box
Barrel: 24" floating barrel; recessed muzzle
Stock & Forearm: Checkered walnut Monte Carlo one-piece pistol grip stock & forearm; cheekpiece; low profile sling studs; recoil pad on magnum
Estimated Value: $280.00 - $375.00

Browning A-Bolt

Browning A-Bolt Stalker

Browning A-Bolt 22

Browning A-Bolt & A-Bolt Hunter
Caliber: 22-250 Rem., 257 Roberts, 7mm-08 Rem., 25-06 Rem., 243 Win., 270 Win., 7mm Rem. magnum, 300 Win. magnum, 30-06 Spring., 308 Win., 338 Win. magnum, or 375 H&H
Action: Bolt action; hammerless; repeating; short or long action
Magazine: Hinged floorplate with detachable box; 4-shot; 3-shot in magnum
Barrel: 22" or 24" blued
Stock & Forearm: Checkered walnut, one-piece pistol grip stock & forearm; swivels; recoil pad on magnum
Estimated Value: $300.00 - $375.00

Browning A-Bolt Stalker
Similar to the A-Bolt except in three special finishes: Stainless Stalker has matte stainless steel finish with graphite fiberglass composite stock (add 5%); Camo Stalker has multi-laminated wood stock with various shades of black & green, matte blue finish; Composite Stalker has graphite/fiberglass composite stock
Estimated Value: $245.00 - $310.00

Browning A-Bolt 22
Similar to the A-Bolt except: 22 long rifle caliber; 5 or 15-shot clip; 22" barrel; add $120.00 for Gold Medallion model
Estimated Value: $230.00 - $290.00

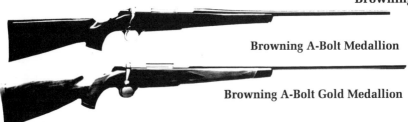

Browning A-Bolt Medallion

Browning A-Bolt Gold Medallion

Browning A-Bolt Medallion
Caliber: 22-250 Rem., 223 Rem., 257 Roberts, 7mm-08 Rem., 25-06 Rem., 243 Win., 270 Win., 280 Rem., 284 Win., 7mm Rem. magnum, 300 Win. magnum, 30-06 Springfield, 308 Win., 338 Win. magnum, or 375 H&H
Action: Bolt action; hammerless; repeating; short or long action
Magazine: Hinged floorplate with detachable box 4-shot; 3-shot magnum
Barrel: 22" or 26" blued; free-floating
Stock & Forearm: Checkered select high-gloss walnut, one-piece pistol grip stock & forearm; rosewood fore-end; swivels; recoil pad on magnum
Estimated Value: $350.00 - $440.00

Browning A-Bolt Gold Medallion
Similar to the A-Bolt Medallion except: higher grade of select walnut; grip palm swell; high cheekpiece; fluted comb. Brass spacers are placed between stock and recoil pad, pistol grip and cap, and fore-end and tip; engraving covers flat sides of receiver and "Gold Medallion" on right side
Estimated Value: $350.00 - $435.00

Browning A-Bolt Micro Medallion
A scaled down version of the A-Bolt Medallion series. Shorter length of pull, shorter barrel, and slimmer overall proportions; 20" barrel; 3-shot magazine (4 in 223 Rem.)
Estimated Value: $350.00 - $435.00

Browning BL-22

Browning BL-22 Grade II

Browning BL-22 Grade II
Similar to BL-22 except: engraving; gold plated trigger; checkered stock & forearm
Estimated Value: $205.00 - $260.00

Browning BL-22
Caliber: 22 short, long, or long rifle (any combination)
Action: Lever action; short throw lever; exposed hammer
Magazine: Tubular; 15 long rifles; 17 longs; 22 shorts
Barrel: Blued; 20"
Stock & Forearm: Plain walnut straight grip stock & forearm; barrel band
Estimated Value: $180.00 - $225.00

Browning

Browning Model 92

Browning BLR, '81 BLR
Caliber: 243, 308, 358, 22-250 Rem., 222, 223 Rem., 257 Roberts, or 7mm-08 Rem.
Action: Lever action; exposed hammer; repeating
Magazine: 4-shot removable box
Barrel: Blued; 20"
Stock & Forearm: Checkered walnut straight grip stock & forearm; recoil pad; barrel band
Estimated Value: $300.00 - $375.00

Browning Model 92, B-92
Caliber: 44 magnum or 357 magnum (added in 1982)
Action: Lever action; exposed three position hammer; repeating
Magazine: 11-shot tubular
Barrel: 20" round
Stock & Forearm: Plain walnut straight grip stock & forearm; barrel band; an authentic remake of the 1892 Winchester designed by John Browning
Estimated Value: $240.00 - $300.00

Browning Model 1895

Browning Model 1885
Caliber: 223 Rem., 22-250 Rem., 270 Win., 30-06 Springfield, 7mm Rem. magnum, or 45-70 Gov't
Action: Falling block, lever action; single shot
Magazine: None; single shot
Barrel: 28" octagon; blued
Stock & Forearm: Checkered walnut straight grip stock & lipped forearm; recoil pad; based on John Browning's Winchester 1885
Estimated Value: $465.00 - $580.00

Browning Model 1895
Caliber: 30-06 Springfield
Action: Lever action; exposed hammer; repeating
Magazine: 5-shot non-detachable box
Barrel: 24"
Stock & Forearm: Walnut straight grip stock & lipped forearm; Higher Grade has checkered stock with engraved steel gray receiver; add 30% for Higher Grade
Estimated Value: $360.00 - $450.00

Browning Model 1886 Limited Edition

Browning Model 1886
Limited Edition High Grade

Browning Model 1886
Caliber: 45-70 Gov't
Action: Lever action; exposed hammer; repeating
Magazine: 8-shot tubular, side-port loading
Barrel: 26"; octagon
Stock & Forearm: Smooth walnut straight-grip stock & forearm; metal, crescent butt plate; checkered stock on higher grade; add 35% for Higher Grade
Estimated Value: $380.00 - $475.00

Browning Model 1886 Ltd. Edition
Caliber: 45-70 Gov't
Action: Lever action; exposed hammer; repeating
Magazine: 8-shot tubular, side-port loading
Barrel: 22"; round
Stock & Forearm: Select walnut straight-grip stock & forearm; metal, crescent butt plate; a limited edition carbine based on the Winchester Model 1886 designed by John Browning; add 35% for Higher Grade
Estimated Value: $450.00 - $560.00

Browning Model BPR

Browning Model 53 Limited Edition
Caliber: 32-20 Win., round nose or hollow point only
Action: Lever action; exposed hammer; repeating
Magazine: 7-shot tubular, side-port loading
Barrel: 22"; round
Stock & Forearm: Checkered, high-gloss walnut straight-grip stock & forearm; a limited edition version of the Winchester Model 53 designed by Browning
Estimated Value: $380.00 - $475.00

Browning Model BPR
Caliber: 22 long rifle or 22 Win. mag.
Action: Slide action; hammerless; repeating; slide release on trigger guard
Magazine: 15-shot tubular; 11-shot in magnum
Barrel: 20¼"
Stock & Forearm: Checkered walnut pistol grip stock & slide handle
Estimated Value: $160.00 - $200.00

Browning Model BPR Grade II
Similar to the model BPR except: magnum only; engraved squirrels & rabbits on receiver
Estimated Value: $230.00 - $300.00

Browning

Browning 22 Semi-Automatic Grade I

Browning 22 Semi-Automatic Grade I
Caliber: 22 short or long rifle
Action: Browning semi-automatic; hammerless; bottom ejection
Magazine: Tubular in stock; 11 long rifles; 16 shorts
Barrel: Blued; 22¼" in long rifle; 19¼" in 22 short
Stock & Forearm: Hand checkered walnut pistol grip stock & forearm; add 40% for FN
Estimated Value: $205.00 - $260.00

Browning 22 Semi-Automatic Grade II
Same as the Grade I except: chrome plated receiver & gold plated trigger; receiver is engraved with squirrel scene; add 40% for FN
Estimated Value: $260.00 - $325.00

Browning 22 Semi-Automatic Grade III
Same as the Grade II except: engraving of bird dog & birds, high-quality finish; add 40% for FN
Estimated Value: $540.00 - $675.00

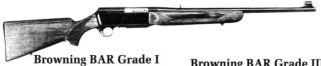

Browning BAR Grade I

Browning BAR Grade I
Caliber: 243 Win., 270 Win., 280 Rem., 308 Win., 30-06, 7mm Rem. magnum, 300 Win. magnum, or 338 Win. magnum
Action: Semi-automatic gas operated; side ejection; hammerless
Magazine: 4-shot; 3-shot in magnum
Barrel: Blued; 22" or 24"
Stock & Forearm: Checkered walnut pistol grip stock & forearm; swivels; recoil pad on mags; add 7% for magnum calibers
Estimated Value: $380.00 - $475.00

Browning BAR Grade II
Engraved version of BAR Grade I; add $50.00 for magnum
Estimated Value: $440.00 - $550.00

Browning BAR Grade III
Similar to BAR Grade I except: elaborate engraving featuring antelope head; discontinued early 1970's. Reintroduced in 1979 with rams & elk engravings; add $60.00 for magnum
Estimated Value: $720.00 - $900.00

Browning Model BAR Grade IV
Similar to Grade I except: elaborate engraving of two running antelope & running deer; magnum has moose & elk engravings; add 5% for magnum
Estimated Value: $1,100.00 - $1,375.00

Browning BAR Grade V
Similar to other Grades of BAR except: this is the fanciest model
Estimated Value: $2,200.00 - $2,750.00

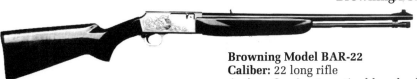

Browning Model BAR-22 Grade II

Browning Model BAR-22 Grade II
Same as the BAR-22 except:
engraved receiver, squirrels & rabbits
Estimated Value: $195.00 - $260.00

Browning Model BAR-22
Caliber: 22 long rifle
Action: Semi-automatic; blow back;
hammerless; repeating
Magazine: 15-shot tubular
Barrel: 20"; recessed muzzle
Stock & Forearm: Checkered walnut
pistol grip stock & forearm; fluted
comb
Estimated Value: $160.00 - $200.00

BSA

BSA Model 12

BSA Model 13 Sporting
Similar to Model 13 except: 22
Hornet caliber
Estimated Value: $225.00 - $300.00

BSA Model 13
Similar to Model 12 except: 25"
barrel
Estimated Value: $200.00 - $250.00

BSA Model 12
Caliber: 22 long rifle
Action: Martini-type
Magazine: None; single shot
Barrel: 29"; blued
Stock & Forearm: Checkered walnut
straight grip stock & forearm; swivels
Estimated Value: $200.00 - $275.00

BSA Model 15
Caliber: 22 long rifle
Action: Martini-type
Magazine: None; single shot
Barrel: Blued; 29"
Stock & Forearm: Walnut stock &
forearm; cheekpiece; swivels
Estimated Value: $300.00 - $375.00

BSA Model 12/15
Similar to Model 12 & 15 in pre-war
& post-war models
Estimated Value: $240.00 - $300.00

BSA Model 12/15

BSA Model 12/15 Heavy Barrel
Similar to Model 12/15 with heavy
barrel
Estimated Value: $260.00 - $325.00

BSA Centurion
Similar to Model 15 except: a
special barrel guaranteed to produce
accurate groups
Estimated Value: $280.00 - $360.00

BSA

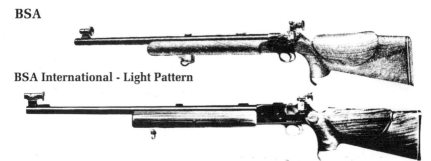

BSA International - Light Pattern

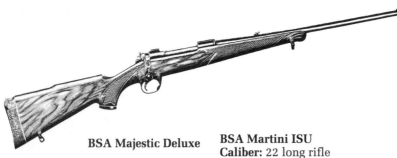

BSA International - Heavy Pattern
Caliber: 22 long rifle
Action: Martini-type
Magazine: None; single shot
Barrel: Blued; 29"; heavy
Stock & Forearm: Match style pistol grip stock with cheekpiece, wide forearm; hand stop; swivels
Estimated Value: $400.00 - $500.00

BSA International - Light Pattern
Similar to Heavy Pattern but lighter weight with a 26" barrel
Estimated Value: $320.00 - $400.00

BSA International Mark III

BSA International Mark II
Similar to Heavy & Light Patterns (choice of barrel); Stock & forearm changed slightly
Estimated Value: $335.00 - $415.00

BSA International Mark III
Similar to Heavy Pattern with different stock & forearm; alloy frame; floating barrel
Estimated Value: $380.00 - $475.00

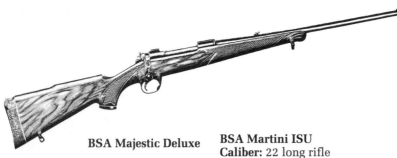

BSA Majestic Deluxe

BSA Majestic Deluxe
Caliber: 22 Hornet, 222, 243, 30-06, 308 Win., or 7x57 mm
Action: Mauser-type bolt action; repeating
Magazine: 4-shot box
Barrel: Blued; 22"
Stock & Forearm: Checkered walnut Monte Carlo one-piece pistol grip stock & lipped forearm; swivels; cheekpiece; recoil pad
Estimated Value: $255.00 - $320.00

BSA Martini ISU
Caliber: 22 long rifle
Action: Martini-type
Magazine: None; single shot
Barrel: Blued; 28"
Stock & Forearm: Match-style walnut pistol grip; adjustable butt plate
Estimated Value: $430.00 - $540.00

BSA Mark V
Similar to ISU except: heavier barrel
Estimated Value: $450.00 - $560.00

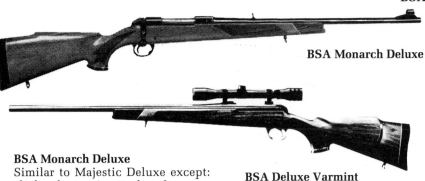

BSA Monarch Deluxe

BSA Monarch Deluxe
Similar to Majestic Deluxe except:
slight change in stock & forearm;
has a recoil pad
Estimated Value: $240.00 - $300.00

BSA Deluxe Varmint

BSA Deluxe Varmint
Similar to Monarch Deluxe with a
heavier 24" barrel
Estimated Value: $250.00 - $310.00

BSA Majestic Deluxe Featherweight
Similar to Majestic Deluxe except:
recoil reducer in barrel. Available in
some magnum calibers; add 20% for
458 Win. magnum caliber
Estimated Value: $255.00 - $320.00

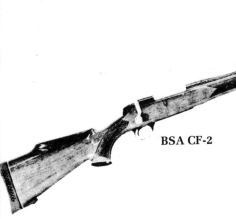

BSA CF-2

BSA Imperial
Caliber: 22 Hornet, 222, 243, 257
Roberts, 270 Win., 7x57mm, 300
Savage, 30-06, or 308 Win.
Action: Bolt action; repeating
Magazine: 4-shot box
Barrel: Blued; 22"; recoil reducer
Stock & Forearm: Checkered walnut
Monte Carlo one-piece pistol grip
stock & lipped forearm; cheekpiece
Estimated Value: $260.00 - $325.00

BSA CF-2
Caliber: 222 Rem., 22-250, 243 Win.,
6.5x55, 7mm Mauser, 7x64, 270
Win., 308 Win., 30-06, 7mm Rem.
mag., or 300 Win. mag.
Action: Bolt action; repeating
Magazine: 4 or 5-shot box; 3-shot in
magnum
Barrel: Blued; 23½"; 24" heavy barrel
in some calibers; add 8% for
magnum calibers with heavy barrel
Stock & Forearm: Checkered walnut
Monte Carlo one-piece pistol grip
stock & forearm; cheekpiece; con-
trasting fore-end tip & grip cap;
swivels; recoil pad; European style
has oil finish; add 14% for European
style; American style has polyeure-
thane finish with white spacers
Estimated Value: $270.00 - $360.00

Carl Gustaf

Carl Gustaf Grade II

Carl Gustaf Grade III

Carl Gustaf Swede

Carl Gustaf Varmint Target

Carl Gustaf Grade III Magnum
Similar to Grade II Magnum except:
select wood; more checkering; high-
quality finish
Estimated Value: $480.00 - $600.00

Carl Gustaf Grade II
Caliber: 22-250, 243, 25-06, 270,
6.5x55, 30-06, or 308
Action: Bolt action; repeating
Magazine: 5-shot staggered column
Barrel: Blued; 23½"
Stock & Forearm: Checkered walnut
Monte Carlo one-piece pistol grip
stock & forearm; swivels
Estimated Value: $380.00 - $475.00

Carl Gustaf Grade II Magnum
Similar to Grade II except magnum
calibers; recoil pad; 3-shot magazine
Estimated Value: $400.00 - $500.00

Carl Gustaf Grade III
Similar to Grade II except: select
wood; more checkering; high-quality
finish
Estimated Value: $460.00 - $575.00

Carl Gustaf Swede
Similar to Grade II except: lipped
forearm but lacking the Monte Carlo
stock
Estimated Value: $400.00 - $500.00

Carl Gustaf Swede Deluxe
Similar to Grade III with lipped
forearm
Estimated Value: $480.00 - $600.00

Carl Gustaf Varmint Target
Caliber: 22-250, 222, 243, or 6.5x55
Action: Bolt action; repeating; large
bolt knob
Magazine: 5-shot staggered column
Barrel: Blued; 27"
Stock & Forearm: Plain walnut
Monte Carlo one-piece pistol grip
stock & forearm
Estimated Value: $375.00 - $500.00

Charles Daly

Charles Daly Hornet

Charles Daly Hornet
Caliber: 22 Hornet
Action: Bolt action; double triggers
Magazine: 5-shot box
Barrel: 24"
Stock & Forearm: Checkered walnut one-piece stock & forearm; also marketed under the name Herold Rifle
Estimated Value: $675.00 - $900.00

Charter Arms

Charter Arms AR-7

Charter Arms AR-7 Explorer
Caliber: 22 long rifle
Action: Semi-automatic
Magazine: 8-shot clip
Barrel: 16"; steel lined aluminum; black or silvertone
Stock & Forearm: Fiberglass, pistol grip stock (no forearm); stock acts as case for gun when dismantled; also available in camouflage; made by Armalite from about 1960 to 1973
Estimated Value: $100.00 - $130.00

Colt

Colt Colteer 1-22

Colt Colteer 1-22
Caliber: 22 short, long, or long rifle
Action: Bolt action; hammerless
Magazine: None; single shot
Barrel: Blued; 20" or 22"
Stock & Forearm: Plain walnut Monte Carlo pistol grip stock & forearm
Estimated Value: $75.00 - $95.00

Colt Coltsman Standard
Caliber: 300 H & H magnum or 30-06
Action: Mauser-type, bolt action; repeating
Magazine: 5-shot box
Barrel: Blued; 22"
Stock & Forearm: Checkered walnut one-piece pistol grip stock & tapered forearm; swivels
Estimated Value: $270.00 - $360.00

Colt

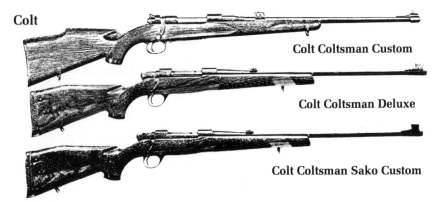

Colt Coltsman Custom

Colt Coltsman Deluxe

Colt Coltsman Sako Custom

Colt Coltsman Custom
Similar to the Coltsman Deluxe except: select wood; cheekpiece; engraving
Estimated Value: $355.00 - $470.00

Colt Coltsman Deluxe
Similar to the Coltsman Standard except: higher quality wood & finish; Monte Carlo stock
Estimated Value: $300.00 - $400.00

Colt Coltsman Sako-Short
Caliber: 222, 222 magnum, 243, or 308
Action: Short Sako-type bolt action; repeating
Magazine: 5-shot box
Barrel: Blued; 22"
Stock & Forearm: Checkered walnut Monte Carlo pistol grip stock & tapered forearm; swivels
Estimated Value: $260.00 - $350.00

Colt Coltsman Deluxe Sako-Short
Similar to Coltsman Sako-Short except: higher quality finish; in calibers 243 or 308 only
Estimated Value: $320.00 - $400.00

Colt Colstman Custom Sako-Short
Similar to Coltsman Deluxe Sako-Short except: select wood; cheekpiece; engraving
Estimated Value: $345.00 - $450.00

Colt Coltsman Sako-Medium
Caliber: 243 or 308 Win.
Action: Medium stroke, Sako-type bolt action; repeating
Magazine: 5-shot box
Barrel: Blued; 24"
Stock & Forearm: Checkered walnut Monte Carlo one-piece pistol grip stock & tapered forearm
Estimated Value: $290.00 - $360.00

Colt Coltsman Custom Sako-Medium
Similar to the Coltsman Sako-Medium except: higher quality finish & recoil pad
Estimated Value: $340.00 - $425.00

Colt Coltsman Sako-Long
Caliber: 264, 270 Win., 300 H&H, 30-06, or 375 H&H
Action: Long stroke, Sako-type bolt action; repeating
Magazine: 5-shot box
Barrel: Blued; 24"
Stock & Forearm: Checkered walnut one-piece pistol grip stock & tapered forearm; swivels
Estimated Value: $300.00 - $375.00

Colt Coltsman Custom Sako-Long
Similar to Coltsman Sako-Long except: higher quality finish; recoil pad; Monte Carlo stock
Estimated Value: $335.00 - $420.00

Colt Sauer Grand African

Colt Sauer-Sporting

Colt Sauer Grand Alaskan
Similar to the Colt Sauer except:
chambered for 375 H&H only;
adjustable rear, hooded ramp front
sights
Estimated Value: $750.00 - $1,000.00

Colt Sauer
Caliber: 25-06, 270, 30-06, 300 Win.
mag., 7mm Rem. mag., 300 Weatherby
mag., 375 H&H mag., or 458 Win. mag;
add $50.00 for mag.
Action: Long stroke, Sauer-type bolt
action; repeating
Magazine: 5-shot detachable box
Barrel: Blued; 24"
Stock & Forearm: Checkered walnut
Monte Carlo one-piece pistol grip
stock & tapered forearm; swivels;
recoil pad
Estimated Value: $765.00 - $950.00

Colt Sauer Grand African
Similar to the Colt Sauer except:
higher quality finish; adjustable
sights; 458 Win. caliber only
Estimated Value: $860.00 - $1,075.00

Colt Sauer-Sporting
Similar to the Colt Sauer except:
short stroke action; chambered for
22-250, 243, or 308 calibers
Estimated Value: $710.00 - $945.00

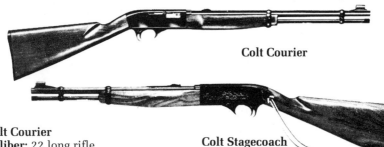

Colt Courier

Colt Stagecoach

Colt Courier
Caliber: 22 long rifle
Action: Semi-automatic
Magazine: 15-shot tubular
Barrel: Blued; 19½"
Stock & Forearm: Plain walnut
straight grip stock & forearm; barrel
band
Estimated Value: $85.00 - $110.00

Colt Stagecoach
Similar to the Colt Courier except:
engraving; 16½" barrel; saddle ring
with leather string
Estimated Value: $95.00 - $120.00

Colt Lightning

Colt AR-15, AR-15A2, AR-15A2 Carbine
Caliber: 223 or 9mm
Action: Gas operated semi-automatic
Magazine: 5-shot clip (223 cal.); 20-shot clip (9mm cal.)
Barrel: 20" with flash supressor; 16" with collapsible stock; also heavy barrel optional
Stock & Forearm: Pistol grip; fiberglass shoulder stock & handguard; swivels; carrying handle; collapsible stock optional in both calibers; add 10% for collapsible stock (AR-15A2)
Estimated Value: $460.00 - $580.00

Colt AR-15 A2 Delta H-Bar
Similar to the AR-15 A2 except: 20" heavy barrel, 3x9 rubber armored variable power scope, removable cheekpiece, leather military style sling & aluminum carrying case
Estimated Value: $815.00 - $1,020.00

Colt Lightning
Caliber: 22 short or long
Action: Slide action; exposed hammer; repeating
Magazine: Tubular; 15 longs, 16 shorts
Barrel: Blued; 24" round or octagon
Stock & Forearm: Plain walnut straight pistol grip stock & checkered slide handle
Estimated Value: $520.00 - $650.00

FN

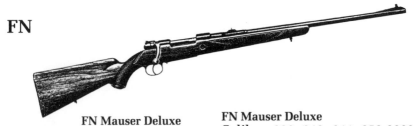

FN Mauser Deluxe

FN Mauser Deluxe Presentation
Similar to the Mauser Deluxe except: Monte Carlo stock; engraving; select wood
Estimated Value: $640.00 - $800.00

FN Mauser Deluxe
Caliber: 220, 243, 244, 250-3000, 270, 7mm, 300, 308, or 30-06
Action: Mauser-type bolt action; repeating
Magazine: 5-shot box
Barrel: Blued; 24"
Stock & Forearm: Checkered one-piece pistol grip stock & forearm; swivels
Estimated Value: $400.00 - $500.00

FN Supreme

FN Supreme Magnum
Similar to the FN Supreme except: 264 mag., 7mm mag., and 300 Win. mag. calibers & 3-shot magazine
Estimated Value: $500.00 - $625.00

FN Supreme
Caliber: 243, 270, 7mm, 30-06, or 308
Action: Mauser-type bolt action; repeating
Magazine: 5-shot box, 4-shot box in 308 or 243 calibers
Barrel: Blued; 22" or 24"
Stock & Forearm: Checkered wood Monte Carlo one-piece pistol grip stock & tapered forearm; cheekpiece; swivels
Estimated Value: $460.00 - $575.00

Harrington & Richardson

Harrington & Richardson 1873 Springfield

Harrington & Richardson Cavalry 171 Deluxe Carbine

H & R 1873
Springfield Commemorative
Caliber: 45-70 Gov't
Action: Trap door
Magazine: None; single shot
Barrel: Blued; 32"
Stock & Forearm: One-piece straight grip stock & full length forearm; barrel band; swivels; replica of the 1873 U.S. Springfield Rifle
Estimated Value: $235.00 - $320.00

H & R Little Big Horn
Commemorative 174
Carbine version of the trap door Springfield, 22" barrel
Estimated Value: $260.00 - $325.00

H & R Cavalry Carbine 171
Similar to the Little Big Horn with saddle ring
Estimated Value: $210.00 - $280.00

H& R Cavalry 171 Deluxe
Same as the Cavalry Carbine 171 except: engraved
Estimated Value: $220.00 - $295.00

Harrington & Richardson

Harrington & Richardson 158 Topper

Harrington & Richardson Mustang

H & R Mustang
Similar to the 158 except: gold plated trigger & hammer; straight grip stock
Estimated Value: $85.00 - $115.00

H & R 158 Topper
Caliber: 22 Hornet, 30-30, 357 magnum, or 44 magnum
Action: Box lock; top lever, break-open; exposed hammer
Magazine: None; single shot
Barrel: Blued; 22"
Stock & Forearm: Hardwood straight or semi-pistol grip stock & forearm; recoil pad
Estimated Value: $85.00 - $110.00

H & R Model 157
Similar to the 158 except: semi-pistol grip stock; full-length forearm; swivels
Estimated Value: $80.00 - $100.00

H & R 158 C, 58 Topper, & 258
Similar to the 158 with extra interchangeable 26" 410 or 20 gauge shotgun barrel; add 18% for nickel finish
Estimated Value: $115.00 - $150.00

H & R Shikari 155
Caliber: 44 magnum or 45-70 Gov't
Action: Single shot; exposed hammer
Magazine: None
Barrel: Blued; 24" or 28"
Stock & Forearm: Wood straight grip stock & forearm; barrel band
Estimated Value: $80.00 - $100.00

Harrington & Richardson Shikari 155

H & R Plainsman 865
Similar to the 765 except: 5-shot clip; 22" barrel
Estimated Value: $70.00 - $90.00

H & R Pioneer 765
Caliber: 22 short, long, or long rifle
Action: Bolt action
Magazine: None; single shot
Barrel: Blued; 24"
Stock & Forearm: Wood Monte Carlo one-piece semi-pistol grip stock & forearm
Estimated Value: $45.00 - $55.00

Harrington & Richardson Pioneer 750

Harrington & Richardson Sahara 755

Harrington & Richardson Model 760

H & R Pioneer 750
Similar to the Pioneer 765; made from the mid 1950's to mid 1980's
Estimated Value: $55.00 - $70.00

H & R Model 751
Similar to the Pioneer 750 except: full-length forearm
Estimated Value: $65.00 - $80.00

H & R Model 866
Similar to the Plainsman 865 except: full-length forearm
Estimated Value: $70.00 - $90.00

H & R Sportster 250
Caliber: 22 long rifle
Action: Bolt action; repeating
Magazine: 5-shot detachable box
Barrel: Blued; 23"
Stock & Forearm: Wood one-piece semi-pistol grip stock & forearm
Estimated Value: $70.00 - $85.00

H & R Model 251
Similar to the Sportster 250 except: special Lyman rear sight
Estimated Value: $75.00 - $90.00

H & R Sahara 755
Caliber: 22 short, long, or long rifle
Action: Blow back; hammerless; single shot; automatic ejector
Magazine: None; single shot
Barrel: Blued; 22"
Stock & Forearm: Monte Carlo one-piece semi-pistol grip stock & full-length forearm
Estimated Value: $65.00 - $80.00

H & R Model 760
Similar to the Sahara 755 except: short forearm
Estimated Value: $55.00 - $70.00

H & R Medalist 450
Caliber: 22 long rifle
Action: Bolt action; repeating
Magazine: 5-shot detachable box
Barrel: Blued; 26"
Stock & Forearm: Target style with pistol grip; swivels
Estimated Value: $110.00 - $140.00

H & R Medalist 451
Similar to the Medalist 450 except: extension rear sight & Lyman front sight
Estimated Value: $125.00 - $155.00

Harrington & Richardson

Harrington & Richardson Model 300

Harrington & Richardson Ultra 301

H & R Model 300
Caliber: 22-250 Rem., 243 Win., 270, 308, 30-06, 300 mag., or 7mm mag.
Action: Mauser-type bolt action; repeating
Magazine: 5-shot box, 3-shot in magnum
Barrel: Blued; 22"
Stock & Forearm: Checkered walnut Monte Carlo one-piece pistol grip stock & forearm; cheekpiece; recoil pad; swivels
Estimated Value: $320.00 - $400.00

H & R Ultra 301
Similar to the Model 300 except: full-length forearm; 18" barrel; no swivels
Estimated Value: $335.00 - $420.00

H & R Model 330
Similar to the Model 300 except: less fancy finish; discontinued in the early 1970's
Estimated Value: $255.00 - $320.00

H & R Model 333
Similar to the Model 330 with no checkering or sights
Estimated Value: $180.00 - $240.00

H & R Fieldsman 852
Caliber: 22 short, long, or long rifle
Action: Bolt action; repeating
Magazine: Tubular: 15 long rifles, 17 longs, 21 shorts
Barrel: Blued; 24"
Stock & Forearm: Plain wood one-piece semi-pistol grip stock & forearm
Estimated Value: $65.00 - $85.00

**Harrington & Richardson
Ultra Wildcat 317**

H & R 317 Presentation
Similar to the Ultra Wildcat 317 except: select wood; special basket-weave checkering
Estimated Value: $440.00 - $550.00

H & R Ultra Wildcat 317
Caliber: 17 Rem., 222, 223, or 17/223 (Handload)
Action: Bolt action, Sako-type; repeating
Magazine: 6-shot box
Barrel: Blued; 24"
Stock & Forearm: Wood Monte Carlo one-piece pistol grip stock & forearm; cheekpiece; recoil pad; swivels
Estimated Value: $400.00 - $500.00

Harrington & Richardson Ultra Medalist 370

Harrington & Richardson Model 340

H & R Ultra Medalist 370
Caliber: 22-250, 243, or 6mm
Action: Sako bolt action; repeating
Magazine: 4-shot box
Barrel: 24" heavy
Stock & Forearm: Monte Carlo one-piece grip stock & forearm; cheekpiece; recoil pad; swivels
Estimated Value: $345.00 - $435.00

H & R Model 340
Caliber: 243 Win., 270 Win., 30-06, 308 Win., or 7mm Mauser (7x57)
Action: Bolt action; repeating; hinged floorplate; adjustable trigger
Magazine: 5-shot
Barrel: Blued; 22"
Stock & Forearm: Checkered walnut one-piece pistol grip stock & forearm; cheekpiece; recoil pad
Estimated Value: $255.00 - $320.00

Harrington & Richardson Model 5200 Match

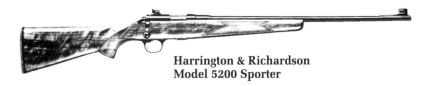

Harrington & Richardson
Model 5200 Sporter

H & R Model 5200 Sporter
Caliber: 22 long rifle
Action: Bolt action; repeating
Magazine: 5-shot clip
Barrel: 24"; recessed muzzle
Stock & Forearm: Checkered walnut one-piece semi-pistol grip stock & forearm; rubber recoil pad
Estimated Value: $260.00 - $325.00

H & R Model 5200 Match
Caliber: 22 long rifle
Action: Bolt action; adjustable trigger
Magazine: None; single shot
Barrel: 28"; heavy target weight; recessed muzzle
Stock & Forearm: Smooth walnut one-piece match-style stock & forearm; swivels; hand stop; rubber recoil pad
Estimated Value: $280.00 - $350.00

Harrington & Richardson

Harrington & Richardson Model 422

Harrington & Richardson Model 749

H & R Model 422
Caliber: 22 short, long, or long rifle
Action: Slide action; hammerless; repeating
Magazine: Tubular: 15 long rifles, 17 longs, 21 shorts
Barrel: Blued; 24"
Stock & Forearm: Plain walnut semi-pistol grip stock & grooved slide handle
Estimated Value: $95.00 - $120.00

H & R Model 749
Caliber: 22 short, long, or long rifle
Action: Slide action; hammerless; repeating
Magazine: Tubular: 18 shorts, 15 longs, 13 long rifles
Barrel: 19"; round; tapered
Stock & Forearm: Plain hardwood pistol grip stock & tapered slide handle
Estimated Value: $85.00 - $110.00

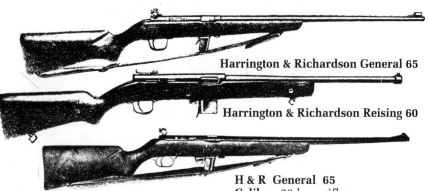

Harrington & Richardson General 65

Harrington & Richardson Reising 60

Harrington & Richardson
Leatherneck 165

H & R General 65
Caliber: 22 long rifle
Action: Semi-automatic
Magazine: 10-shot detachable box
Barrel: Blued; 23"
Stock & Forearm: Wood one-piece semi-pistol grip stock & forearm. Used as a Marine training rifle during World War II
Estimated Value: $240.00 - $300.00

H & R Reising 60
Caliber: 45
Action: Semi-automatic
Magazine: 12 or 20-shot detachable box
Barrel: Blued; 18¼"
Stock & Forearm: Plain wood one-piece semi-pistol grip stock & forearm
Estimated Value: $325.00 - $425.00

H & R Leatherneck 165
Lighter version of the General 65 with ramp front sights
Estimated Value: $110.00 - $140.00

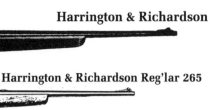

Harrington & Richardson Reg'lar 265

Harrington & Richardson Leatherneck 150

H & R Targeteer Jr.
A youth version of the Targeteer
Special 465 with short stock; 5-shot
magazine; 20" barrel
Estimated Value: $70.00 - $95.00

H & R Reg'lar 265
Similar to the Leatherneck 165
except: bolt action; 22" barrel
Estimated Value: $65.00 - $90.00

H & R Leatherneck 150
Caliber: 22 long rifle
Action: Semi-automatic; hammerless
Magazine: 5-shot detachable box
Barrel: Blued; 22"
Stock & Forearm: Wood one-piece
semi-pistol grip stock & forearm
Estimated Value: $105.00 - $130.00

H & R Ace 365
Similar to the Reg'lar 265 except:
single shot only
Estimated Value: $55.00 - $70.00

H & R Targeteer Special 465
Similar to the Reg'lar 265 except: 25"
barrel; swivels; heavier
Estimated Value: $85.00 - $110.00

H & R Model 151
Similar to the Leatherneck 150
except: special peep rear sight
Estimated Value: $110.00 - $135.00

Harrington & Richardson Model 308

H & R Model 308
Caliber: 243, 264, or 308
Action: Semi-auto; gas operated
Magazine: 3-shot detachable box
Barrel: Blued; 22"
Stock & Forearm: Checkered walnut
Monte Carlo one-piece pistol grip
stock & forearm; cheekpiece; swivels;
became Model 360 in 1967
Estimated Value: $230.00 - $290.00

H & R Lynx 800
Caliber: 22 long rifle
Action: Semi-automatic; hammerless
Magazine: 10-shot clip
Barrel: Blued; 22"
Stock & Forearm: Walnut one-piece
semi-pistol grip stock & forearm
Estimated Value: $70.00 - $90.00

H & R Model 360
Same as the Model 308; made from
1967 to the early 1970's
Estimated Value: $240.00 - $300.00

Harrington & Richardson Model 700 Deluxe

H & R Model 700 Deluxe
Similar to the Model 700 except:
select custom finish; checkering;
cheekpiece; recoil pad; 4X scope
Estimated Value: $195.00 - $260.00

H & R Model 700
Caliber: 22 WMR
Action: Semi-automatic; hammerless
Magazine: 5 or 10-shot detachable
box
Barrel: 22"
Stock & Forearm: Plain walnut
Monte Carlo one-piece pistol grip
stock & forearm
Estimated Value: $140.00 - $175.00

Heckler & Koch

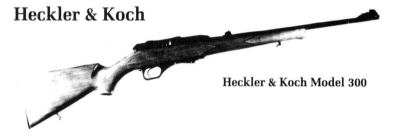

Heckler & Koch Model 300

Heckler & Koch Model 300
Caliber: 22 Win. mag.
Action: Semi-automatic; blow back
design
Magazine: 5 or 15-shot detachable
box
Barrel: Blued; 20"
Stock & Forearm: Checkered walnut
Monte Carlo one-piece pistol grip
stock & lipped forearm; swivels
Estimated Value: $255.00 - $320.00

Heckler & Koch Model 270
Caliber: 22 long rifle
Action: Semi-automatic; blow back
design
Magazine: 5 or 20-shot detachable
box
Barrel: Blued; 20"
Stock & Forearm: Plain walnut, one-
piece semi-pistol grip stock & lipped
forearm
Estimated Value: $185.00 - $230.00

Heckler & Koch Model 91 & 93
Caliber: 223 (Model 93) or 308
(Model 91)
Action: Semi-automatic
Magazine: 25-shot clip (Model 93);
20-shot clip (Model 91); 5-shot clip
available for both rifles
Barrel: 16¼" matte black (Model 93);
17¾" matte black (Model 91)
Stock & Forearm: Matte black, fixed,
high-impact plastic three-piece
stock, forearm & pistol grip; a
retractable metal stock available; add
12% for retractable metal stock
Estimated Value: $560.00 - $700.00

Heckler & Koch Model 94 Carbine
Similar to the Model 91 & Model 93
except: 9mm caliber; 30-shot clip;
16½" barrel; add 12% for retractable
metal stock
Estimated Value: $560.00 - $700.00

Heckler & Koch Model 770

Heckler & Koch Model 630
Caliber: 221, 222, 223 Rem., or 22 Hornet
Action: Semi-automatic
Magazine: 4-shot box; 10-shot available
Barrel: Blued; 18"
Stock & Forearm: Checkered walnut Monte Carlo pistol grip, one-piece stock & lipped forearm; swivels
Estimated Value: $375.00 - $500.00

Heckler & Koch Model 770
Similar to the Model 630 except: 243 or 308 Win. calibers; 20" barrel; 3-shot magazine
Estimated Value: $415.00 - $520.00

Heckler & Koch Model 940
Similar to the Model 630 except: 30-06 Springfield caliber; 22" barrel; 3-shot magazine
Estimated Value: $395.00 - $530.00

Heckler & Koch Model SL-6 & SL-7
Caliber: 223 (SL-6) or 308 (SL-7)
Action: Semi-automatic
Magazine: 4-shot clip (SL-6); 3-shot clip (SL-7); 10-shot clip available for both calibers
Barrel: 17¾"; round; black matte finish
Stock & Forearm: Smooth European one-piece stock & forearm with ventilated wood handguard over barrel
Estimated Value: $420.00 - $525.00

High Standard

High Standard Hi Power

High Standard Flite King
Caliber: 22 short, long, or long rifle
Action: Slide action; hammerless; repeating
Magazine: Tubular: 17 long rifle, 19 long, 24 short
Barrel: Blued; 24"
Stock & Forearm: Checkered walnut Monte Carlo pistol grip stock & grooved slide handle; early models have no checkering
Estimated Value: $95.00 - $115.00

High Standard Hi Power
Caliber: 270 or 30-06
Action: Bolt action; Mauser-type; repeating
Magazine: 4-shot box
Barrel: Blued; 22"
Stock & Forearm: Walnut one-piece semi-pistol grip stock & tapered forearm
Estimated Value: $200.00 - $250.00

High Standard Hi Power Deluxe
Similar to Hi Power except: checkered Monte Carlo stock & swivels
Estimated Value: $225.00 - $280.00

High Standard/Husqvarna

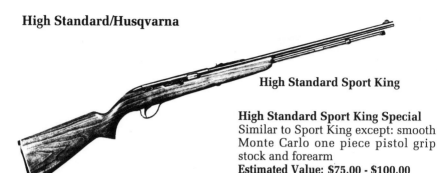

High Standard Sport King

High Standard Sport King Special
Similar to Sport King except: smooth Monte Carlo one piece pistol grip stock and forearm
Estimated Value: $75.00 - $100.00

High Standard Sport King
Caliber: 22 short, long, or long rifle
Action: Semi-automatic
Magazine: Tubular: 15 long rifles, 17 longs, 21 shorts
Barrel: Blued; 22¼"
Stock & Forearm: Checkered or smooth wood, one-piece pistol grip stock & forearm
Estimated Value: $95.00 - $120.00

High Standard Sport King Deluxe
Similar to the Sport King except: checkered Monte Carlo one piece pistol grip stock and forearm
Estimated Value: $95.00 - $125.00

High Standard Sport King Carbine
Carbine version of the Sport King; straight stock; 18¼" barrel; smaller magazine; swivels
Estimated Value: $90.00 - $120.00

Husqvarna

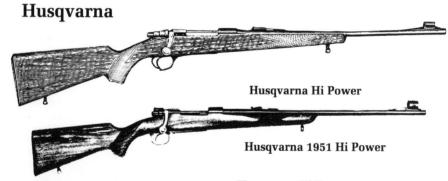

Husqvarna Hi Power

Husqvarna 1951 Hi Power

Husqvarna 1950 Hi Power
Similar to the Hi Power except: 220, 270, or 30-06 caliber only
Estimated Value: $270.00 - $340.00

Husqvarna 1951 Hi Power
Similar to the Hi Power except: higher comb stock
Estimated Value: $280.00 - $350.00

Husqvarna Hi Power
Caliber: 220 Swift, 270, 30-06, 6.5x55, 8x57, or 9.3x57
Action: Mauser-type bolt action; repeating
Magazine: 5-shot box
Barrel: Blued; 23¾"
Stock & Forearm: Checkered beech one-piece pistol grip stock & tapered forearm; swivels
Estimated Value: $260.00 - $325.00

Husqvarna 1100 Hi Power Deluxe

Husqvarna 1000 Super Grade
Similar to the 1100 except: Monte
Carlo stock
Estimated Value: $330.00 - $420.00

Husqvarna 1100 Hi Power Deluxe
Similar to the 1951 Hi Power except:
walnut stock & forearm
Estimated Value: $320.00 - $400.00

Husqvarna 3000 Crown Grade

Husqvarna 3100 Crown Grade

Husqvarna P-3000 Presentation

Husqvarna 6000 Imperial Custom

Husqvarna 3000 Crown Grade
Same as the 3100 Crown Grade
except: Monte Carlo stock
Estimated Value: $350.00 - $465.00

Husqvarna P-3000 Presentation
A fancy version of the 3000 Crown
Grade with engraving; select wood;
adjustable trigger
Estimated Value: $540.00 - $725.00

Husqvarna 3100 Crown Grade
Caliber: 243, 270, 7mm Rem., 30-06,
or 308 Win.
Action: Mauser-type bolt action;
repeating
Magazine: 5-shot box
Barrel: Blued; 23¾"
Stock & Forearm: Checkered walnut
one-piece pistol grip stock & tapered
forearm; swivels
Estimated Value: $350.00 - $440.00

Husqvarna 6000 Imperial Custom
Similar to the 3100 Crown Grade
except: higher quality finish; folding
sight; adjustable trigger
Estimated Value: $395.00 - $525.00

Husqvarna

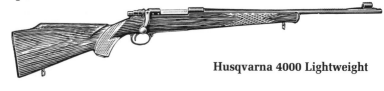

Husqvarna 4000 Lightweight

Husqvarna 4100 Lightweight

Husqvarna 4000 Lightweight
Similar to the 4100 Lightweight except: Monte Carlo stock; no rear sight
Estimated Value: $385.00 - $480.00

Husqvarna 456 Lightweight
Similar to the 4100 Lightweight except: full-length forearm
Estimated Value: $390.00 - $490.00

Husqvarna 4100 Lightweight
Caliber: 243, 270, 7mm, 306, or 308 Win.
Action: Mauser-type bolt action; repeating
Magazine: 5-shot box
Barrel: Blued; 20½"
Stock & Forearm: Checkered walnut one-piece pistol grip stock & tapered forearm
Estimated Value: $365.00 - $460.00

Husqvarna 7000 Imperial Monte Carlo
Similar to the Model 4000 Lightweight except: higher quality wood; lipped forearm; folding sight; adjustable trigger
Estimated Value: $440.00 - $550.00

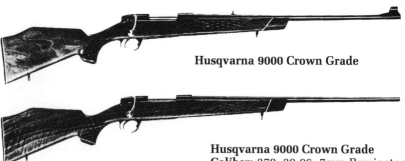

Husqvarna 9000 Crown Grade

Husqvarna 8000 Imperial Grade

Husqvarna 8000 Imperial Grade
Similar to the 9000 Crown Grade except: select wood; engraving; no sights
Estimated Value: $480.00 - $600.00

Husqvarna 9000 Crown Grade
Caliber: 270, 30-06, 7mm Remington mag., or 300 Win. mag.
Action: Bolt action; repeating
Magazine: 5-shot box
Barrel: Blued; 23¾"
Stock & Forearm: Checkered walnut Monte Carlo one-piece pistol grip stock & forearm; swivels
Estimated Value: $390.00 - $490.00

Pocket Guide to Rifles

Husqvarna 610 Varmint

Husqvarna 358 Magnum
Caliber: 358 Norma mag.
Action: Bolt action; repeating
Magazine: 3-shot box
Barrel: Blued; 25½"
Stock & Forearm: Checkered walnut Monte Carlo one-piece pistol grip stock & forearm
Estimated Value: $380.00 - $475.00

Husqvarna 610 Varmint
Caliber: 222
Action: Short stroke bolt action; repeating
Magazine: 4-shot detachable box
Barrel: Blued; 23¾"
Stock & Forearm: Checkered walnut Monte Carlo one-piece pistol grip stock & forearm
Estimated Value: $340.00 - $425.00

Ithaca

Ithaca Model LSA-55

Ithaca Model LSA-55 Deluxe

Ithaca Model LSA-65 Deluxe

Ithaca Model LSA-55
Caliber: 222, 22-250, 6mm, 243, or 308
Action: Bolt action; repeating
Magazine: 3-shot detachable box
Barrel: Blued; 22"
Stock & Forearm: Monte Carlo one-piece pistol grip stock & tapered forearm
Estimated Value: $260.00 - $350.00

Ithaca Model LSA-55 Heavy Barrel
Similar to the LSA-55 except: cheekpiece; recoil pad; heavy barrel
Estimated Value: $320.00 - $400.00

Ithaca Model LSA-55 Deluxe
Similar to the LSA-55 except: checkering; recoil pad
Estimated Value: $295.00 - $390.00

Ithaca Model LSA-65
Similar to Model LSA-55 except: 25-06, 270, or 30-06 caliber; 4-shot magazine
Estimated Value: $280.00 - $375.00

Ithaca Model LSA-65 Deluxe
Similar to Model LSA-55 Deluxe except: in same calibers as the LSA-65
Estimated Value: $300.00 - $400.00

Ithaca

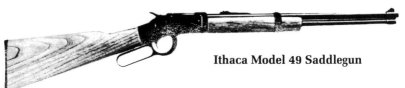

Ithaca Model 49 Saddlegun

Ithaca Model 49 Saddlegun
Caliber: 22 short, long, or long rifle
Action: Lever action; exposed hammer
Magazine: None; single shot
Barrel: Blued; 18"
Stock & Forearm: Plain or checkered wood straight grip stock & forearm; barrel band
Estimated Value: $65.00 - $80.00

Ithaca Model LSA-55 Turkey Gun
Caliber: 222 under 12 gauge full choke
Action: Top lever, break open; exposed hammer
Magazine: None; over/under shot gun & rifle combination
Barrel: 24½"; rifle under full choke shotgun with matted rib
Stock & Forearm: Checkered walnut Monte Carlo pistol grip stock & forearm; recoil pad; swivels
Estimated Value: $360.00 - $450.00

Ithaca Model 49R

Ithaca Model 49 Youth
Similar to Model 49 saddle gun except: shorter stock for young shooters
Estimated Value: $60.00 - $75.00

Ithaca Model 49 Magnum
Similar to Model 49 in 22 magnum rim fire
Estimated Value: $70.00 - $85.00

Ithaca Model 49 Deluxe
Similar to the Model 49 Saddlegun except: checkered stock, gold hammer & trigger; swivels
Estimated Value: $70.00 - $90.00

Ithaca Model 49 Presentation
Similar to Model 49 Deluxe with engraving & nameplate; calibers 22 short, long, long rifle, & 22 magnum rim fire
Estimated Value: $85.00 - $110.00

Ithaca Model 49R (Repeater)
Similar to the Model 49 Saddlegun except: 20" barrel & 15-shot tubular magazine; lever action repeater
Estimated Value: $95.00 - $120.00

Ithaca Model 72 Saddlegun
Caliber: 22 long rifle
Action: Lever action; exposed hammer; repeating
Magazine: 15-shot tubular
Barrel: Blued; 18½"
Stock & Forearm: Plain walnut straight grip stock & forearm; barrel band
Estimated Value: $125.00 - $155.00

Ithaca Model 72 Deluxe

Ithaca Model 72 Magnum
Similar to the Model 72 Saddlegun
except: 22 magnum; magazine holds
11 shots
Estimated Value: $125.00 - $165.00

Ithaca Model 72 Deluxe
Similar to the Model 72 Saddlegun
except: brushed silver receiver;
engraving; octagon barrel
Estimated Value: $130.00 - $175.00

Ithaca Model X5-C
Caliber: 22 long rifle
Action: Semi-automatic; hammerless
Magazine: 7-shot clip
Barrel: Blued; 22"
Stock & Forearm: Wood one-piece
semi-pistol grip stock & forearm
Estimated Value: $105.00 - $130.00

Ithaca Model X5-T
Similar to the Model X5-C except:
16-shot tubular magazine
Estimated Value: $110.00 - $140.00

Iver Johnson

Iver Johnson Model 2X

Iver Johnson Lever Action
Caliber: 22 short, long, long rifle, or
22 Win. mag.; add 7% for mag.
Action: Lever action, side ejection;
exposed hammer
Magazine: Tubular; 21 shorts, 17
longs, 15 long rifles (can be mixed);
12 Win. magnums
Barrel: 18½"; round; blued
Stock & Forearm: Smooth hardwood
stock & forearm; barrel band
Estimated Value: $120.00 - $160.00

Iver Johnson Model X
Caliber: 22 short, long, or long rifle
Action: Bolt action
Magazine: None; single shot
Barrel: Blued; 22"
Stock & Forearm: Wood one-piece
pistol grip stock & forearm
Estimated Value: $70.00 - $100.00

Iver Johnson Model 2X
Similar to the Model X except: 24"
barrel & improved stock
Estimated Value: $85.00 - $110.00

Iver Johnson

Iver Johnson Wagonmaster

Iver Johnson Li'l Champ

Iver Johnson Wagonmaster
Caliber: 22 short, long, long rifle, or 22 magnum; add 12% for magnum
Action: Lever action; repeating
Magazine: Tubular; 21 shorts, 17 longs, 15 long rifles; (can be mixed); 12 Win. magnum
Barrel: Blued; 18¼"
Stock & Forearm: Smooth wood straight grip stock & forearm; barrel band
Estimated Value: $100.00 - $125.00

Iver Johnson Survival Carbine
Caliber: 30 carbine or 223 (5.7mm)
Action: Gas operated semi-automatic
Magazine: 5, 15, or 30-shot detachable clip
Barrel: 18"; blued; stainless steel; add 25% for stainless steel
Stock & Forearm: Hard plastic, one-piece pistol grip stock & forearm; metal handguard; folding stock available; add 20% for folding stock
Estimated Value: $140.00 - $175.00

Iver Johnson Li'l Champ
Caliber: 22 short, long, or long rifle
Action: Bolt action
Magazine: None; single shot
Barrel: Blued; 16¼"
Stock & Forearm: Molded one-piece stock & forearm; nickel plated bolt; designed for young beginners
Estimated Value: $55.00 - $65.00

Iver Johnson Targetmaster
Caliber: 22 short, long, or long rifle
Action: Slide action, repeating
Magazine: Tubular; 19 shorts, 15 longs, 12 long rifles (can be mixed)
Barrel: Blued; 18½"
Stock & Forearm: Smooth hardwood straight grip stock & grooved slide handle
Estimated Value: $100.00 - $125.00

Iver Johnson Trailblazer
Caliber: 22 long rifle
Action: Semi-automatic, hammerless
Magazine: Clip
Barrel: Blued; 18½"
Stock & Forearm: Checkered walnut, one-piece Monte Carlo semi-pistol grip stock & forearm
Estimated Value: $75.00 - $100.00

Pocket Guide to Rifles

Iver Johnson PM 30G

Iver Johnson PM 30G, M1Carbine, & PM30
Caliber: 30 M1 or 223
Action: Gas operated, semi-automatic
Magazine: 15-shot detachable clip; 5 or 30-shot clips available
Barrel: 18"; blued or stainless steel add 20% for stainless steel
Stock & Forearm: Wood, semi-pistol grip one-piece stock & forearm; add 7% for walnut; slot in stock; ventilated metal or wood handguard
Estimated Value: $160.00 - $200.00

Iver Johnson PM30S, Model M1 Sporter
Similar to the M1 Carbine with a wood hand guard & no slot in the stock
Estimated Value: $150.00 - $190.00

Iver Johnson PM30P, Commando or Paratrooper
Similar to the M1 Carbine with pistol grip at rear & at forearm; telescoping wire shoulder stock; add 20% for stainless steel
Estimated Value: $175.00 - $220.00

Iver Johnson Model EW22 HBA & MHBA
Similar to the Model PM30 except: 22 long rifle or 22 win. magnum; add 75% for magnum (MHBA)
Estimated Value: $100.00 - $125.00

Iver Johnson Model 9MM
Similar to the Model PM30 except: 9MM Parabellum; 16" barrel; 20-shot magazine
Estimated Value: $145.00 - $190.00

Johnson

Johnson MMJ Spitfire

Johnson MMJ Spitfire
Caliber: 223
Action: Semi-automatic
Magazine: 5, 15, or 30-shot clip
Barrel: Blued; 18"
Stock & Forearm: Wood one-piece semi-pistol grip stock & forearm; wood hand guard; a conversion of the M1 carbine
Estimated Value: $175.00 - $230.00

Johnson Custom Deluxe Sporter
Similar to the MMJ Spitfire except: Monte Carlo pistol grip stock & rear peep sight
Estimated Value: $185.00 - $240.00

Johnson Folding Stock
Similar to the MMJ Spitfire except: special metal folding shoulder stock
Estimated Value: $190.00 - $250.00

Kimber

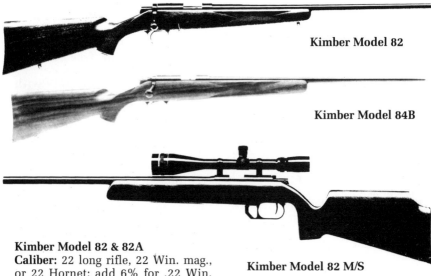

Kimber Model 82

Kimber Model 84B

Kimber Model 82 M/S

Kimber Model 82 & 82A
Caliber: 22 long rifle, 22 Win. mag., or 22 Hornet; add 6% for .22 Win. magnum or .22 Hornet
Action: Bolt action; repeating; rear locking bolt lugs
Magazine: 5-shot detachable box (10-shot available) in 22 long rifle; 4-shot in 22 Win. mag.; 3-shot in 22 Hornet
Barrel: 22½"; blued; light sporter; sporter; target
Stock & Forearm: Checkered walnut, one-piece pistol grip stock & forearm (Classic); optional Monte Carlo stock; swivels; add 10% for Cascade stock; add 33% for Custom Classic stock; add 52% for Super America stock
Estimated Value: $715.00 - $895.00

Kimber Model 82 M/S
Similar in appearance to the Model 82 except: single shot; 20½" heavy barrel; adjustable target trigger; competition stock; 22 long rifle caliber only; this gun is designed for metallic silhouette shooting
Estimated Value: $445.00 - $550.00

Kimber Model 82B
Similar to the Model 82 with internal improvements; available with sporter or varmint barrel; Classic stock standard; add 12% for Cascade stock; add 33% for Custom Classic stock; add 100% for Brownell stock; add 50% for Super America stock; 14% for Continental stock; add 95% for Super Continental stock
Estimated Value: $500.00 - $625.00

Kimber Model 84 & 84A
Similar to the Model 82 except: Mini-Mauser-type action; 223 Rem., 221 Fireball, 222 Rem. mag., 17 Rem., 17 Match IV, 6x47, or 6x45 calibers; add 12% for Cascade stock; add 28% for Custom Classic stock
Estimated Value: $560.00 - $700.00

Kimber Big Game Rifle

Kimber Mini-Classic
Similar to the 82A except: 18" barrel; lipped forearm
Estimated Value: $400.00 - $500.00

Kimber 82A Government
A single shot 22 bolt action target rifle designed for the Army; heavy target barrel & stock; built on the Kimber 82A action
Estimated Value: $360.00 - $445.00

Kimber Model 84B
Similar to the Model 84 with internal improvements; add 12% for Continental stock; 90% for Super Continental; 50% for Super America
Estimated Value: $650.00 - $800.00

Kimber Big Game Rifle
Caliber: 270 Win., 280 Rem., 7mm Rem. magnum, 30-06, 300 Win. magnum, 338 Win. magnum, 375 H&H, or 416 Rigby (African model)
Action: Bolt action, repeating, combining features of the pre-'64 Winchester Model 70 & Mauser 98
Magazine: 5-shot in calibers 270, 280 & 30-06; 3-shot in calibers 7mm mag., 300 mag., 338 mag., 375 H&H, & 416 Rigby
Barrel: 22½" featherweight barrel in 270, 280, & 30-06; 24" medium barrel in 7mm, 300, & 338; 24" heavy barrel in 375 H&H & 416 Rigby
Stock & Forearm: Checkered walnut one-piece pistol grip stock & forearm; black forearm tip; swivels; add 6% for magnum; add 11% for 375 H&H; add 30% for Custom Classic; add 11% for Super America; add 100% for African Model (416 Rigby)
Estimated Value: $1,075.00 - $1,350.00

Kleinguenther

Kleinguenther K-14

Kleinguenther MV 2130
Caliber: 243, 270, 30-06, 300 mag., 308, or 7mm Rem.
Action: Mauser-type bolt action, repeating
Magazine: 2-shot box
Barrel: Blued; 25"
Stock & Forearm: Checkered walnut Monte Carlo one-piece pistol grip stock & tapered forearm; recoil pad
Estimated Value: $440.00 - $550.00

Kleinguenther K-14
Caliber: 243, 270, 30-06, 300 mag. 308, 7mm Rem., 25-06, 7x57, or 375 H&H
Action: Bolt action
Magazine: Hidden clip, 3-shot
Barrel: Blued; 24"or 26"
Stock & Forearm: Checkered walnut one-piece pistol grip stock & tapered forearm; recoil pad
Estimated Value: $480.00 - $600.00

Kleinguenther/Mannlicher

Kleinguenther K-15 Insta-fire

Kleinguenther Model K-22
Caliber: 22 long rifle or 22 Magnum
Action: Bolt action; repeating; adjustable trigger
Magazine: 5-shot hidden clip
Barrel: 21½" chrome-poly steel
Stock & Forearm: Checkered beechwood, Monte Carlo pistol grip one-piece stock & forearm; swivels; add 16% for magnum, 30% for deluxe, 110% for deluxe custom
Estimated Value: $210.00 - $260.00

Kleinguenther K-15 Insta-fire
Caliber: 243, 25-06, 270, 30-06, 308 Win., 308 Norma mag., 300 Win. mag., 7mm Rem. mag., 375 H&H, 7x57, 270 mag., 300 Weath. mag., or 257 Weath. mag.
Action: Bolt action; repeating; adjustable trigger
Magazine: 5-shot hidden clip; 3-shot in magnum
Barrel: 24"; 26" in magnum
Stock & Forearm: Checkered walnut Monte Carlo one-piece pistol grip stock & forearm; several shade choices; rosewood fore-end & cap; swivels; engraving & select wood at additional cost; add $50.00 for magnum
Estimated Value: $765.00 - $960.00

Mannlicher

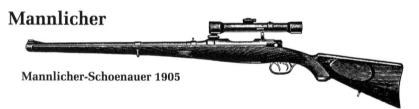

Mannlicher-Schoenauer 1905

Mannlicher-Schoenauer 1903
Caliber: 6.5 x 53mm
Action: Bolt action; repeating; double set trigger; "butter knife" style bolt handle
Magazine: 5-shot rotary
Barrel: Blued; 17¾"
Stock & Forearm: Walnut semi-pistol grip stock & tapered, full-length forearm; swivels; cheekpiece
Estimated Value: $760.00 - $950.00

Mannlicher-Schoenauer 1908
Similar to the 1903 except: 19¾" barrel in 7x57 & 8x56mm calibers
Estimated Value: $700.00 - $875.00

Mannlicher-Schoenauer 1910
Similar to the 1903 except: 19¾" barrel; 9.5x56mm caliber
Estimated Value: $720.00 - $900.00

Mannlicher-Schoenauer 1924
Similar to the 1903 except: 19¾" barrel; 30-06 caliber
Estimated Value: $840.00 - $1,050.00

Mannlicher-Schoenauer 1905
Similar to the 1903 except: 19¾" barrel; 9x56mm caliber
Estimated Value: $720.00 - $900.00

Mannlicher

Mannlicher-Schoenauer 1952 Carbine

Mannlicher-Schoenauer High Velocity

Mannlicher-Schoenauer 1950 Sporter

Mannlicher-Schoenauer 1950 Carbine

Mannlicher-Schoenauer 1950 Carbine
Similar to the 1950 Sporter except:
20" barrel & full-length forearm
Estimated Value: $660.00 - $830.00

Mannlicher-Schoenauer High Velocity
Caliber: 7x64, 30-06, 8x60, 9.3x62, or 10.75x68
Action: Bolt action; repeating; "butter knife" bolt handle
Magazine: 5-shot rotary
Barrel: Blued; 23¾"
Stock & Forearm: Checkered walnut one-piece pistol grip stock & tapered forearm; cheekpiece; swivels
Estimated Value: $780.00 - $975.00

Mannlicher-Schoenauer 1950-6.5
Similar to the 1950 Carbine except:
18" barrel; 6.5x53mm caliber
Estimated Value: $680.00 - $850.00

Mannlicher-Schoenauer 1952 Sporter
Similar to the 1950 Sporter except:
slight changes in stock; slanted bolt handle
Estimated Value: $775.00 - $970.00

Mannlicher-Schoenauer 1950 Sporter
Caliber: 257, 270 Win., or 30-06
Action: Bolt action; repeating; "butter knife" bolt handle
Magazine: 5-shot rotary
Barrel: Blued; 24"
Stock & Forearm: Checkered walnut one-piece pistol grip stock & tapered forearm; cheekpiece; swivels
Estimated Value: $755.00 - $950.00

Mannlicher-Schoenauer 1952 Carbine
Similar to 1952 Sporter except: 20" barrel; full-length forearm
Estimated Value: $765.00 - $960.00

Mannlicher-Schoenauer 1952 - 6.5
Similar to 1952 Carbine except: 18" barrel; 6.5x53mm caliber
Estimated Value: $720.00 - $900.00

Mannlicher

Mannlicher-Schoenauer 1956 Sporter

Mannlicher-Schoenauer 1961 MCA

Mannlicher-Schoenauer 1961 MCA Carbine

Mannlicher-Schoenauer 1956 Carbine
Similar to the 1956 Sporter except: 20" barrel; full-length forearm; also addition of calibers 6.5mm, 257, 270, 7mm, or 308
Estimated Value: $630.00 - $790.00

Mannlicher-Schoenauer 1956 Sporter
Caliber: 243 or 30-06
Action: Bolt action; repeating; "butter knife" slanted bolt handle
Magazine: 5-shot rotary
Barrel: Blued; 22"
Stock & Forearm: Checkered walnut pistol grip stock & forearm; high comb; cheekpiece; swivels
Estimated Value: $600.00 - $760.00

Mannlicher-Schoenauer 1961 MCA
Similar to the 1956 Sporter except: Monte Carlo stock
Estimated Value: $640.00 - $800.00

Mannlicher-Schoenauer 1961 MCA Carbine
Similar to the 1956 Carbine except: Monte Carlo stock
Estimated Value: $680.00 - $850.00

Steyr-Mannlicher SL Carbine

Steyr-Mannlicher SL Carbine
Similar to the Model SL except: 20" barrel & full-length forearm
Estimated Value: $1,050.00 - $1,300.00

Steyr-Mannlicher Model SL
Caliber: 222 Rem., 222 Rem. magnum, 223 Rem., or 5.6x50 magnum
Action: Bolt action; repeating
Magazine: 5-shot rotary
Barrel: Blued; 23½"
Stock & Forearm: Checkered walnut Monte Carlo pistol grip, one-piece stock & tapered forearm; recoil pad; swivels
Estimated Value: $970.00 - $1,215.00

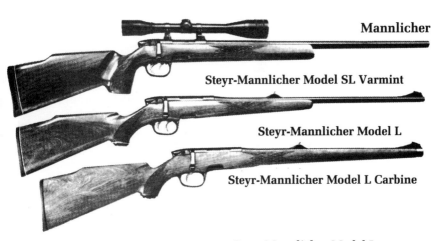

Steyr-Mannlicher Model SL Varmint

Steyr-Mannlicher Model L

Steyr-Mannlicher Model L Carbine

Steyr-Mannlicher Model SL Varmint
Similar to the Model SL except: 26" heavy barrel; 222 Rem. or 223 Rem. calibers only
Estimated Value: $1,050.00 - $1,300.00

Steyr-Mannlicher Model L Carbine
Similar to the Model L except: 20" barrel; full-length forearms
Estimated Value: $1,050.00 - $1,300.00

Steyr-Mannlicher Model L
Similar to the Model SL except: 22-250 Rem., 5.6x57, 6mm Rem., 7mm, 243 Win., or 308 Win. calbers only
Estimated Value: $970.00 - $1,215.00

Steyr-Mannlicher Model L Varmint
Similar to the Model L except: varmint stock; 26" heavy barrel; 22-250 Rem., 243 Win. or 308 Win. calbers only
Estimated Value: $1,050.00 - $1,300.00

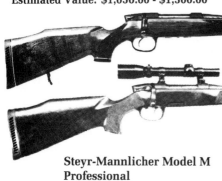

Steyr-Mannlicher Model M

Steyr-Mannlicher Model M Professional

Steyr-Mannlicher Model M Professional
Similar to the Model M except: parkerized metal finish; ABS Cycolac stock; 23½" barrel only
Estimated Value: $820.00 - $1,025.00

Steyr-Mannlicher Model M
Caliber: 6.5x55, 7x64, 270 Win., 30-06, 25-06 Rem.; 7x57, or 9.3x62
Action: Bolt action; repeating
Magazine: 5-shot rotary
Barrel: Blued; 20" on full stock models; 23½" on half stock models
Stock & Forearm: Checkered walnut Monte Carlo pistol grip stock; standard or full-length forearm; swivels; add 8% for full stock
Estimated Value: $ 970.00 - $1,215.00

Mannlicher

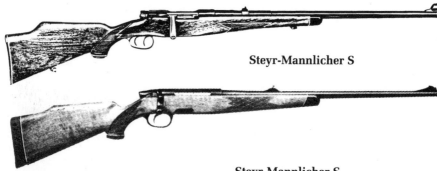

Steyr-Mannlicher S

Steyr-Mannlicher S/T, Tropical

Steyr-Mannlicher S/T, Tropical
Similar to the Model S except: heavy barrel; 375 H&H mag., 9.3x64, or 458 Win. mag. calibers only; add $50.00 for buttstock magazine
Estimated Value: $1,120.00 - $1,400.00

Steyr-Mannlicher S
Similar to Model M except: 26" barrel in magnum calibers; 7mm Rem., 257 Weath., 264 Win. 6.5x68, 300 H&H, 300 Win., 338 Win., 375 H&H & 458 Win. Half stock only; butt magazine optional; add $50.00 for buttstock 4-shot magazine
Estimated Value: $1,050.00 - $1,300.00

Mannlicher-Schoenauer M-72 LM Carbine

Steyr-Mannlicher ML 79 Luxus
Caliber: 7x57, 7x64, 270 Win., 30-06 Springfield; others available on request
Action: Bolt action; short stroke; repeating
Magazine: 3-shot detachable; 6-shot optional
Barrel: 23½"; 20" on full stock model
Stock & Forearm: Checkered European walnut Monte Carlo one-piece pistol grip stock & forearm; swivels; full-length stock optional; add 6% for full-length stock or 6-shot magazine
Estimated Value: $1,270.00 - $1,580.00

Mannlicher-Schoenauer M-72 & M-72S
Caliber: 22-250, 5.6x57, 243, 6.5x57, 6mm, 7x57, or 270
Action: Bolt action; repeating
Magazine: 5-shot rotary
Barrel: Blued; 23½"
Sights: Open rear, ramp front
Stock & Forearm: Checkered walnut one-piece pistol grip stock & tapered forearm; cheekpiece; recoil pad; swivels
Estimated Value: $640.00 - $800.00

Mannlicher-Schoenauer M-72 LM Carbine
Similar to M-72 except: 20" barrel; full-length forearm
Estimated Value: $660.00 - $825.00

Steyr-Mannlicher Model SSG Match

Steyr-Mannlicher Model SSG Marksman
Caliber: 308 Win., 7.62x51, or 243 Win.
Action: Bolt action; repeating
Magazine: 5-shot
Barrel: 26"; heavy barrel optional
Stock & Forearm: Checkered European walnut one-piece stock & forearm; recoil pad; ABS Cycolac stock optional; deduct 20% for ABS Cycolac stock
Estimated Value: $1,250.00 - $1,560.00

Steyr-Mannlicher Model SSG Match
A match rifle similar to the SSG Marksman except: heavy barrel; peep sight; stippled checkering; hand stop; deduct 12% for ABS Cycolac stock
Estimated Value: $1,385.00 - $1,725.00

Mark X

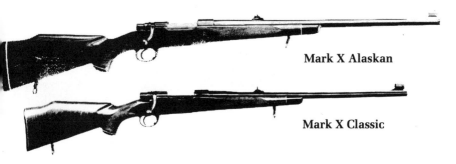

Mark X Alaskan

Mark X Classic

Mark X Alaskan
Caliber: 375 H & H or 458 Win. mag.
Action: Mauser-type bolt action; repeating; adjustable trigger
Magazine: 3-shot box with hinged floor plate
Barrel: Blued; 24"
Stock & Forearm: Checkered, select walnut, Monte Carlo pistol grip, one-piece stock & forearm; recoil pad; swivels
Estimated Value: $360.00 - $450.00

Mark X Classic
Caliber: 22-250, 25-06, 243, 270, 308, 30-06, 7mm mag., 7x57, or 300 Win. mag.
Action: Mauser-type; Bolt action; repeating; adjustable trigger
Magazine: 3-shot box with hinged floor plate
Barrel: 24"
Stock & Forearm: Checkered walnut Monte Carlo one-piece pistol grip stock & forearm; swivels
Estimated Value: $280.00 - $350.00

Mark X

Mark X Mini Mark X

Mark X Viscount
Similar to the Mark X Classic except: special hammer-forged, chrome vanadium steel barrel; add $20.00 for magnum calibers
Estimated Value: $325.00 - $400.00

Mark X LT. WT.
Similar to the Viscount except: lightweight Carbolite stock; 270, 30-06, or 7mm Rem. magnum calibers; add $20.00 for magnum
Estimated Value: $315.00 - $390.00

Mark X Cavalier
Similar to the Mark X Classic except: fancier stock; recoil pad
Estimated Value: $320.00 - $400.00

Mark X Mini Mark X
Caliber: 223 or 7.62x39
Action: Bolt action; repeating; Mauser action scaled down for 223 caliber
Magazine: 5-shot
Barrel: Blued; 20"
Stock & Forearm: Checkered walnut, Monte Carlo one-piece pistol grip stock & forearm
Estimated Value: $300.00 - $375.00

Mark X Whitworth Express

Mark X Marquis
Caliber: 243, 270, 7x57mm, 308, or 30-06
Action: Bolt action; Mauser-type; repeating
Magazine: 5-shot box with hinged floor plate
Barrel: 20"
Stock & Forearm: Checkered walnut Monte Carlo one-piece full-length pistol grip stock & forearm; swivels
Estimated Value: $300.00 - $375.00

Mark X Continental
Similar to the Marquis except: "butter knife" bolt handle & double set triggers
Estimated Value: $320.00 - $400.00

Mark X Whitworth Express, Safari
Caliber: 37.5 H&H mag. or 458 Win. mag.
Action: Bolt action; Mauser style; repeating; adjustable trigger
Magazine: 3-shot box with hinged floor plate
Barrel: 24"
Stock & Forearm: Checkered European walnut, Monte Carlo one-piece stock & forearm; swivels; recoil pad
Estimated Value: $540.00 - $675.00

Marlin Model 80

Marlin Model 80E

Marlin Model 80DL

Marlin Garfield Model 80G

Marlin Model 80 & 80E
Caliber: 22 short, long, or long rifle
Action: Bolt action; takedown type; repeating
Magazine: 8-shot detachable box
Barrel: 24"
Stock & Forearm: Plain pistol grip stock & forearm
Estimated Value: $70.00 - $85.00

Marlin Model 80C
Similar to the Model 80 except: slight improvements; forearm is semi-beavertail; replaced by the 80G in 1960
Estimated Value: $70.00 - $90.00

Marlin Model 80DL
Same as the Model 80C except; swivels; hooded front sight; peep rear sight
Estimated Value: $70.00 - $90.00

Marlin Model 80G
Same as the Model 80C; made from about 1960 to 1966
Estimated Value: $65.00 - $85.00

Marlin Model 65 & 65E
Caliber: 22 short, long, or long rifle
Action: Bolt action
Magazine: None; single shot
Barrel: 24" round
Stock & Forearm: Pistol grip stock & grooved forearm
Estimated Value: $60.00 - $75.00

Marlin

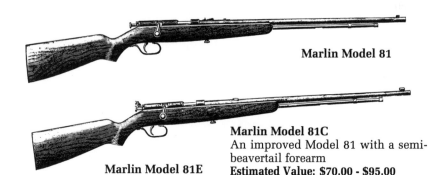

Marlin Model 81

Marlin Model 81E

Marlin Model 81C
An improved Model 81 with a semi-beavertail forearm
Estimated Value: $70.00 - $95.00

Marlin Model 81 & 81E
Caliber: 22 short, long, or long rifle
Action: Bolt action; repeating
Magazine: Tubular; 24 shorts, 20 longs, 18 long rifles
Barrel: 24"
Stock & Forearm: Plain pistol grip stock & forearm
Estimated Value: $75.00 - $90.00

Marlin Model 81 DL
Same as Model 81C exept it has swivels; hooded front sight, peep rear sight
Estimated Value: $80.00 - $100.00

Marlin Glenfield Model 81G
Basically the same as the Marlin Model 81C; produced as the 81G from about 1960 to 1965
Estimated Value: $70.00 - $90.00

Marlin Model 100

Marlin Model 100
Caliber: 22 short, long, or long rifle
Action: Bolt action
Magazine: None; single shot
Barrel: 24" round
Stock & Forearm: Plain pistol grip stock & forearm
Estimated Value: $55.00 - $70.00

Marlin Model 100S
Tom Mix Special
Same as Model 100 except: hooded front sight, peep rear sight; made from 1937 to 1942
Estimated Value: $160.00 - $175.00

Marlin Model 100 SB
Same as Model 100 except: smooth bore for use with shot cartridges
Estimated Value: $65.00 - $80.00

Marlin Model 100G; Glenfield 10
Basically same as the Marlin Model 100
Estimated Value: $50.00 - $60.00

Marlin Model 101 & 101-DL
Basically same as Model 100 except; beavertail forearm; Peep rear, hooded front sights on 101-DL
Estimated Value: $70.00 - $90.00

Marlin Model 15

Marlin Model 15, 15Y, & 15YN
Caliber: 22 short, long, or long rifle
Action: Bolt action
Magazine: None; single shot
Barrel: 22" round, 16¼" on 15Y & 15YN
Stock & Forearm: Checkered hardwood, Monte Carlo pistol grip one-piece stock & forearm; 15Y & 15YN are for young shooters.
Estimated Value: $90.00 - $110.00

Marlin Model 2000 Target
Caliber: 22 long rifle
Action: Bolt action; thumb safety; red cocking indicator
Magazine: None (5-shot Summer Biathlon kit available)
Barrel: Heavy, 22" selected Micro-groove with match chamber and recessed muzzle
Stock & Forearm: High-comb fiberglass/Kevlar stock with stipple-finish forearm; stock butt plate adjustable for length of pull, height, & angle
Estimated Value: $330.00 - $410.00

Marlin Model 422 Varmint King

Marlin Model 322 Varmint
Caliber: 222 Rem.
Action: Bolt action (Sako Short, Mauser); repeating
Magazine: 3-shot clip
Barrel: 24"
Stock & Forearm: Checkered hardwood stock & forearm. Made for about 3 years
Estimated Value: $290.00 - $360.00

Marlin Model 422 Varmint King
Caliber: 222 Rem.
Action: Bolt action; repeating
Magazine: 3-shot detachable clip
Barrel: 24" round
Stock & Forearm: Checkered Monte Carlo pistol grip stock & forearm; replaced the Model 322 about 1958 but was discontinued after one year
Estimated Value: $300.00 - $380.00

Marlin

Marlin Model 455 Sporter

Marlin Model 122 Target Rifle
Caliber: 22 short, long, or long rifle
Action: Bolt action
Magazine: None; single shot
Barrel: 22"; round
Stock & Forearm: Wood Monte Carlo pistol grip stock & forearm; swivels
Estimated Value: $70.00 - $85.00

Marlin Model 455 Sporter
Caliber: 270, 30-06, or 308
Action: Bolt action; FN Mauser action with Sako trigger
Magazine: 5-shot box
Barrel: 24"; round stainless steel
Stock & Forearm: Checkered wood Monte Carlo stock & forearm
Estimated Value: $300.00 - $375.00

Marlin Model 781

Marlin Model 780
Caliber: 22 short, long, or long rifle
Action: Bolt action; repeating
Magazine: 7-shot clip
Barrel: 22"; Blued
Stock & Forearm: Checkered walnut Monte Carlo one-piece semi-pistol grip stock & forearm
Estimated Value: $95.00 - $120.00

Marlin Glenfield 20, 25, 25N, 25M & 25MN
Caliber: 22 long rifle or 22 Win. mag. (25MN)(25M)
Action: Bolt action; Repeating; thumb safety
Magazine: 7-shot clip
Barrel: 22"; round, blued
Stock & Forearm: Plain or checkered walnut, semi-pistol grip stock & plain forearm; Model 25N has no checkering; produced from about 1966 to the early 1980's as Model 20; currently sold as Model 25N; add 15% for magnum (25M, 25MN)
Estimated Value: $95.00 - $115.00

Marlin Model 781
Same as Model 780 except tubular magazine; 25 shorts, 19 longs, 17 long rifles
Estimated Value: $100.00 - $125.00

Marlin Model 980
Caliber: 22 Win. mag.
Action: Bolt action; repeating
Magazine: 8-shot clip
Barrel: Blued; 24" round
Stock & Forearm: Monte Carlo one-piece stock & forearm; swivels
Estimated Value: $80.00 - $100.00

Marlin Model 782

Marlin Model 783

Marlin Model 783
Same as Model 782 except: 12-shot
tubular magazine
Estimated Value: $120.00 - $150.00

Marlin Model 782
Caliber: 22 Win. magnum
Action: Bolt action; repeating
Magazine: 7-shot clip
Barrel: 22"
Stock & Forearm: Monte Carlo one-
piece semi-pistol grip stock &
forearm
Estimated Value: $130.00 - $160.00

Marlin Model 880

Marlin Model 881
Same as the Model 880 except: 22
short, long, or long rifle; tubular
magazine, holds 25 shorts, 19 longs
or 17 long rifle
Estimated Value: $135.00 - $165.00

Marlin Model 880
Caliber: 22 long rifle
Action: Bolt action; thumb safety,
red cocking indicator
Magazine: 7-shot clip
Barrel: 22"; Blued; micro-groove
rifling
Stock & Forearm: Monte Carlo pistol
grip checkered walnut one-piece
stock & forearm; swivel studs &
rubber rifle butt pad
Estimated Value: $130.00 - $160.00

Marlin Model 882 & 882L
Same as the Model 880 except: 22
Win. magnum only; add 6% for
laminated stock
Estimated Value: $140.00 - $175.00

Marlin Model 883 & 883N
Same as the Model 880 except: 12-
shot tubular magazine; add 10% for
nickel plate (883N)
Estimated Value: $145.00 - $180.00

Marlin

Marlin Model 92

Marlin Model 93

Marlin Model 92
Caliber: 22 short, long, or long rifle; 32 short or long, rim fire or center fire
Action: Lever action; exposed hammer
Magazine: Tubular, under barrel; 22 caliber - 25 shorts, 20 longs, & 28 long rifles; 32 caliber - 17 shorts & 14 longs; 16" barrel magazine holds 15 shorts, 12 longs, 10 long rifles
Barrel: 16", 24", 26", or 28" round or octagon; blued
Stock & Forearm: Plain walnut straight grip stock & forearm; also known as Model 1892
Estimated Value: $425.00 - $500.00

Marlin Model 93
Caliber: 25-36 Marlin, 30-30, 32 Special, 32-40, or 38-55
Action: Lever action; exposed hammer; repeating
Magazine: 10-shot tubular; under barrel
Barrel: 26"-32"; round or octagon
Stock & Forearm: Plain walnut straight grip stock & forearm; also known as Model 1893
Estimated Value: $525.00 - $650.00

Marlin Model 93 Carbine
Basically same as the Model 93 except: produced in 30-30 & 32 special calibers only; standard carbine sights; 20" round barrel; 7-shot magazine
Estimated Value: $550.00 - $675.00

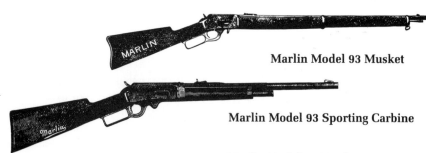

Marlin Model 93 Musket

Marlin Model 93 Sporting Carbine

Marlin Model 93 Sporting Carbine
Same as Model 93 Carbine except: smaller magazine holds 5 shots
Estimated Value: $540.00 - $670.00

Marlin Model 93 Musket
Same as the Model 93 except: 30" standard barrel; equipped with a musket stock; military forearm; ramrod; angular bayonet
Estimated Value: $750.00 - $900.00

Marlin

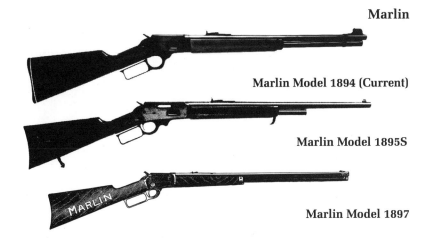

Marlin Model 1894 (Current)

Marlin Model 1895S

Marlin Model 1897

Marlin Model 1894 & 1894S
Caliber: 25-20, 32-30, 38-40; current model is 44 magnum (1970's to present); 41 mag. added 1984; 45 long Colt added 1988; 41 magnum & 45 long Colt dropped in 1990
Action: Lever action; exposed hammer; repeating. Hammer block safety added 1986
Magazine: 10-shot; tubular
Barrel: Round or octagon, 20", 24"-32"; 20" on current models
Stock & Forearm: Plain walnut straight or pistol grip stock & forearm
Estimated Value:
    1970's & later: $265.00 - $335.00
    Early (1894-1935): $600.00 - $700.00

Marlin Model 1894CL
Similar to the current model 1894S except: 25-20, 32-30 , or 318 Bee; 6-shot magazine; 22" barrel
Estimated Value: $285.00 - $355.00

Marlin Model 1894C, 1894CS, 1894M
Similar to the current model 1894S except: 357 magnum caliber; 18½" barrel; 9-shot magazine
Estimated Value: $265.00 - $330.00

Marlin Model 1895
Caliber: 33 WCF, 38-56, 40-65, 40-70, 40-82, or 45-70
Action: Lever action; exposed hammer; repeating
Magazine: 9-shot; tubular
Barrel: 24"; octagon or round; blued
Stock & Forearm: Walnut straight or pistol grip stock & forearm
Estimated Value: $580.00 - $725.00

Marlin Model 1895S, 1895SS
Similar to the Model 1895 except: introduced in the late 1970's; 45-70 gov't caliber; 22" barrel; 4-shot magazine; swivels
Estimated Value: $285.00 - $360.00

Marlin Model 1897
Caliber: 22 short, long, or long rifle
Action: Lever action; exposed hammer; repeating
Magazine: 25 shorts, 20 longs, or 18 long rifles in full length magnum; 16 shorts, 12 longs, or 10 long rifles in half length mag.; tubular
Barrel: 16", 24", 26", or 28"; blued
Stock & Forearm: Plain walnut straight or pistol grip stock & forearm
Estimated Value: $370.00 - $450.00

Marlin

Marlin Model 36

Marlin Model 36 Sporting Carbine

Marlin Model 36 Sporting Carbine
Same as Model 36A except: lighter weight; 20" barrel
Estimated Value: $260.00 - $325.00

Marlin Model 36
Caliber: 30-30, or 32 Special
Action: Lever action; exposed hammer; repeating
Magazine: 6-shot tubular
Barrel: 20"; round; blued
Stock & Forearm: Pistol grip stock & semi-beavertail forearm; carbine barrel band
Estimated Value: $240.00 - $300.00

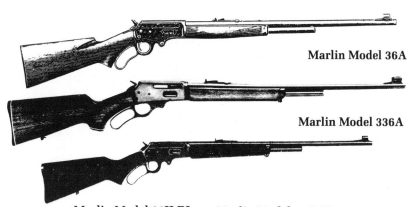

Marlin Model 36A

Marlin Model 336A

Marlin Model 36H-DL

Marlin Model 36A
Same as Model 36 except: 24" barrel; ⅔ magazine; weighs slightly more
Estimated Value: $240.00 - $300.00

Marlin Model 336A & 336A-DL
Basically the same as Model 36A except: rounded breech bolt & improved action; checkered stock & forearm; swivels on 336A-DL
Estimated Value: $185.00 - $230.00

Marlin Model 36H-DL
Same as Model 36A except: stock & forearm are checkered; swivels
Estimated Value: $240.00 - $300.00

Marlin Model 336C Carbine & 336CS
This is basically the same as the Model 36 except: round breech bolt & improved action; also 35 Remington & 375 Winchester calibers; hammer block safety added in 1986
Estimated Value: $235.00 - $295.00

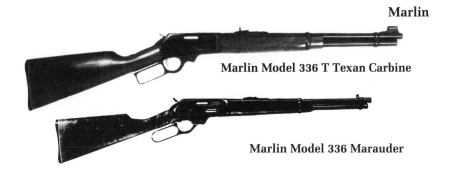

Marlin Model 336 T Texan Carbine

Marlin Model 336 Marauder

Marlin Model 336T
Texan Carbine & 336TS
Same as Model 336C except: straight stock; 18½" barrel; never produced in 32 caliber; but was available from 1963 to 1967 in 44 magnum; produced from 1953 to 1987 in 30-30 caliber
Estimated Value: $200.00 - $250.00

Marlin Model 336 Marauder
Same as Model 336T except: lighter weight; 16¼" barrel
Estimated Value: $210.00 - $255.00

Marlin Model 336 ER
Similar to the Model 336 C except: 356 Winchester or 308 Winchester calibers; recoil pad; swivels & strap
Estimated Value: $220.00 - $275.00

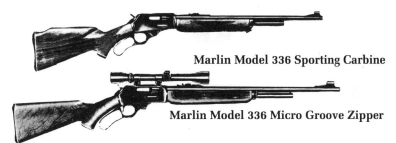

Marlin Model 336 Sporting Carbine

Marlin Model 336 Micro Groove Zipper

Marlin Model 336 LTS
Similar to the Model 336TS except: 30-30 Win. caliber; 16¼" barrel; rubber butt pad
Estimated Value: $210.00 - $260.00

Marlin Model 336 Sporting Carbine
Same as Model 336A except: lighter weight; 20" barrel
Estimated Value: $160.00 - $200.00

Marlin Model 336 Micro Groove Zipper
Caliber 219 Zipper; otherwise same rifle as Model 336A
Estimated Value: $280.00 - $350.00

Marlin Model 336 Zane Grey Century
Same basic rifle as Model 336A except: 22" octagon barrel; brass fore-end cap; brass butt plate & medallion in receiver; 10,000 were produced in 1972.
Estimated Value: $240.00 - $300.00

Marlin

Marlin Model 39

Marlin Model 39A

Marlin Model 39A Mountie

Marlin Model 39M

Marlin Model 39A
Same as Model 39 except: round barrel; heavier stock; semi-beavertail forearm; production began about 1938; replaced by the golden 39A in 1958
Estimated Value: $175.00 - $220.00

Marlin Model 39M
Similar to 39A except: 20" barrel; less magazine capacity; straight grip stock
Estimated Value: $150.00 - $190.00

Marlin Model 39
Caliber: 22 short, long, or long rifle
Action: Lever action; exposed hammer; repeating; takedown-type
Magazine: 25 shorts, 20 longs, 18 long rifles; tubular under barrel
Barrel: 24"; octagon
Stock & Forearm: Plain pistol grip stock & forearm
Estimated Value: $260.00 - $325.00

Marlin Model 39A Mountie
Same as Model 39 except: straight grip, lighter stock; 20" barrel; produced from 1950's to 1960
Estimated Value: $155.00 - $195.00

Marlin Model 39M Golden Mountie

Marlin Model 39M Golden Mountie
Same as Model 39A Mountie except:
gold-plated trigger; magazine
capacity 21 shorts, 16 longs or 15
long rifles; produced from 1950's to
1988
Estimated Value: $185.00 - $230.00

Marlin Model Golden 39A

Marlin Model 444

Marlin Model 39TDS
Similar to the Model 39AS except:
smaller; 16½" barrel; tubular
magazine holds 16 shorts, 13 longs,
or 11 long rifles; comes with
floatable zippered case; assembles
without tools
Estimated Value: $250.00 - $315.00

Marlin Model Golden 39A & 39AS
Caliber: 22 short, long, or long rifle
Action: Lever-action; exposed hammer; takedown-type; gold-plated trigger; 39AS (added in 1988) has hammer block safety & rebounding hammer
Magazine: 25 shorts, 20 longs, or 18 long rifle; tubular, under barrel
Barrel: 24"; micro-groove, round barrel
Stock & Forearm: Plain Walnut pistol grip stock & forearm
Estimated Value: $235.00 - $295.00

Marlin Model 444, 444S & 444SS
Caliber: 444 Marlin
Action: Action-lever; repeating; Hammer block safety added 1986 (444S); currently called 444SS
Magazine: 4-shot tubular
Barrel: Blued; 24" micro-groove
Stock & Forearm: Monte Carlo straight or pistol grip stock; carbine-type forearm; barrel band; swivels
Estimated Value: $285.00 - $355.00

Marlin

Marlin Glenfield Model 30

Marlin Model 375

Marlin Glenfield Model 30
Caliber: 30-30 Win.
Action: Lever action; repeating
Magazine: 6-shot tubular
Barrel: Blued; 20" round
Stock & Forearm: Walnut, plain or checkered; semi-pistol grip stock & forearm
Estimated Value: $155.00 - $195.00

Marlin Glenfield Model 30GT
Similar to the Glenfield 30 except: straight grip stock & 18½" barrel
Estimated Value: $150.00 - $190.00

Marlin Glenfield Model 30A & Marlin 30AS
Similar to the Glenfield 30; made from the late 1970's; plain stock on the 30AS
Estimated Value: $200.00 - $250.00

Marlin Model 375
Caliber: 375 Win.
Action: Lever-action; side ejection; repeating
Magazine: 5-shot tubular
Barrel: 20" round, blued
Stock & Forearm: Plain walnut pistol grip stock & forearm with fluted comb; swivels
Estimated Value: $240.00 - $300.00

Marlin Model 57

Marlin Model 56 Levermatic
Caliber: 22 short, long, or long rifle
Action: Lever-action; repeating
Magazine: 8-shot clip
Barrel: Blued; 22" round
Stock & Forearm: Monte Carlo pistol grip stock
Estimated Value: $120.00 - $150.00

Marlin Model 57
Caliber: 22 short, long, or long rifle
Action: Lever action; repeating
Magazine: Tubular, under barrel; 19 long rifles, 21 longs, 27 shorts
Barrel: Blued; 22" round
Stock & Forearm: Plain Monte Carlo pistol grip stock & forearm
Estimated Value: $130.00 - $160.00

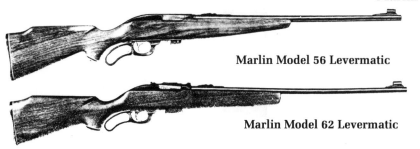

Marlin Model 56 Levermatic

Marlin Model 62 Levermatic

Marlin Model 57M Levermatic
Caliber: 22 Win. mag.
Action: Lever action; repeating
Magazine: 15-shot tubular; under barrel
Barrel: 24" round, blued
Stock & Forearm: Monte Carlo pistol grip stock
Estimated Value: $130.00 - $165.00

Marlin Model 62 Levermatic
Caliber: 256 mag. (1963 to 1966); 30 carbine (1966 to 1969)
Action: Lever action; repeating
Magazine: 4-shot clip
Barrel: Blued; 23" round
Stock & Forearm: Monte Carlo pistol grip stock
Estimated Value: $160.00 - $210.00

Marlin Model 20

Marlin Model 18 Baby Slide Action

Marlin Model 20 & 20 S
Caliber: 22 short, long, or long rifle
Action: Slide action; exposed hammer; repeating
Magazine: 25 shorts, 20 longs, 18 long rifles in full length, or 15 shorts, 12 longs, 10 long rifles in half-length; tubular, under barrel
Barrel: Blued; 24" octagon
Stock & Forearm: Plain walnut straight grip stock & grooves slide handle
Estimated Value: $250.00 - $315.00

Marlin Model 18 Baby Slide Action
Caliber: 22 short, long, or long rifle
Action: Slide action; exposed hammer; repeating
Magazine: Tubular, under barrel; 15 shorts, 12 longs, 10 long rifles
Barrel: Blued; 20" round or octagon
Stock & Forearm: Plain walnut straight grip stock & slide handle
Estimated Value: $260.00 - $320.00

Marlin Model 29
Similar to Model 20 except: round 23" barrel; plain slide handle; half-length magazine only
Estimated Value: $225.00 - $290.00

Marlin

Marlin Model 25

Marlin Model 27

Marlin Model 25
Caliber: 22 short & 22 CB caps only
Action: Slide action; exposed hammer; repeating
Magazine: 15-shot tubular, under barrel
Barrel: Blued; 23" octagon
Stock & Forearm: Plain walnut straight grip stock & slide handle; this takedown model was made for about 1 year in 1909 or 1910.
Estimated Value: $260.00 - $325.00

Marlin Model 27 & 27S
Caliber: 25-20, 32-30, & 25 Stevens RF (1920 to 1932) (27S)
Action: Slide action; exposed hammer; repeating
Magazine: 6-shot; ⅔ tubular, under barrel
Barrel: Blued; 24" octagon
Stock & Forearm: Plain walnut straight grip stock & grooved slide handle
Estimated Value: $250.00 - $315.00

Marlin Model 32

Marlin Model 38

Marlin Model 38
Caliber: 22 short, long, or long rifle
Action: Slide action; exposed hammer; repeating
Magazine: 15 shorts, 12 longs, 10 long rifles; ⅔ tubular, under barrel
Barrel: Blued; 24" octagon or round
Stock & Forearm: Plain pistol grip stock & grooved slide handle
Estimated Value: $250.00 - $310.00

Marlin Model 32
Caliber: 22 short, long, or long rifle
Action: Slide action; concealed hammer; repeating
Magazine: 25 shorts, 20 longs, 18 long rifles in full length, or 15 shorts, 12 longs, 10 long rifles in ⅔ length; tubular, under barrel
Barrel: Blued; 24" octagon
Stock & Forearm: Walnut pistol grip stock & grooved slide handle; produced for one year about 1914
Estimated Value: $265.00 - $330.00

Marlin Model 37

Marlin Model 47

Marlin Model 47
Basically same as the Model 37, it was used as a bonus give away with purchase of Marlin Stocks; discontinued in 1931 after six years production
Estimated Value: $360.00 - $450.00

Marlin Model 37
Caliber: 22 short, long, or long rifle
Action: Slide action; exposed hammer; repeating
Magazine: 25 shorts, 20 longs, 18 long rifles; tubular, under barrel
Barrel: 24"; round blued
Stock & Forearm: Walnut pistol grip stock & forearm
Estimated Value: $240.00 - $300.00

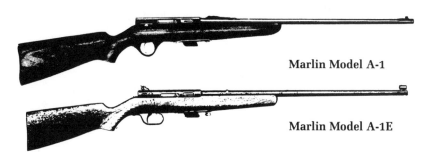

Marlin Model A-1

Marlin Model A-1E

Marlin Model 50

Marlin Model A-1 & A-1E
Caliber: 22 long rifle
Action: Semi-auto; side ejection
Magazine: 6-shot detachable box
Barrel: 24"; blued; A-1E has peep sight
Stock & Forearm: Plain pistol grip one piece stock & forearm
Estimated Value: $105.00 - $130.00

Marlin Model 50 & 50E
Caliber: 22 long rifle
Action: Semi-automatic; takedown model; side ejection
Magazine: 6-shot detachable box
Barrel: 24"; round, blued; 50E has peep sight
Stock & Forearm: Plain pistol grip one piece stock & grooved forearm
Estimated Value: $90.00 - $110.00

Model A-1C & A-1DL
An improved Model A-1; semi-beavertail forearm; produced from about 1940 for six years; peep sight & swivels on A-1DL
Estimated Value: $125.00 - $155.00

Marlin

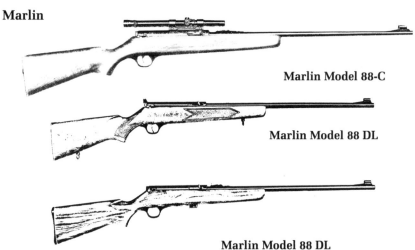

Marlin Model 88-C

Marlin Model 88 DL

Marlin Model 89-C

Marlin Model 88-C
Caliber: 22 long rifle
Action: Semi-automatic; side ejection
Magazine: 14-shot tubular, in stock
Barrel: Blued; 24" round
Stock & Forearm: Pistol grip one piece stock and forearm
Estimated Value: $80.00 - $100.00

Marlin Model 88 DL
Same as Model 88-C except checkered stock, swivels & peep sight; produced for three years beginning about 1953
Estimated Value: $90.00 - $110.00

Marlin Model 89-C & 89-DL
Same as Model 88-C except: magazine is 7 or 12-shot clip; has tapered forearm; model 89-DL has swivels & peep sight
Estimated Value: $70.00 - $90.00

Marlin Model 98

Marlin Model 98
Caliber: 22 long rifle
Action: Semi-automatic; side ejection
Magazine: 15-shot tubular
Barrel: 22"; blued, round
Stock & Forearm: Walnut Monte Carlo pistol grip one piece stock and forearm
Estimated Value: $85.00 - $105.00

Marlin Model 99
Caliber: 22 long rifle
Action: Semi-automatic; side ejection
Magazine: 18-shot tubular
Barrel: 22"; round, blued
Stock & Forearm: Plain pistol grip one piece stock & forearm
Estimated Value: $75.00 - $95.00

Pocket Guide to Rifles

Marlin Model 99DL

Marlin Glenfield Model 99G

Marlin Model 99C

Marlin Model 99DL
Same as Model 99C except: swivels
& jeweled breech bolt; made for five
years beginning about 1960.
Estimated Value: $85.00 - $105.00

Marlin Model 99C
Same as Model 99 except: Monte
Carlo one piece stock an forearm
(some are checkered); gold-plated
trigger; grooved receiver
Estimated Value: $80.00 - $100.00

Marlin Glenfield Model 99G
Basically same as the Marlin Model
99 except: plain stock
Estimated Value: $65.00 - $80.00

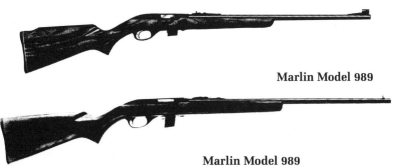

Marlin Model 989

Marlin Glenfield Model 989G

Marlin Model 989
Caliber: 22 long rifle only
Action: Semi-automatic; side
ejection
Magazine: 7-shot clip
Barrel: 22"; blued, round
Stock & Forearm: Monte Carlo pistol
grip one piece stock & forearm
Estimated Value: $80.00 - $105.00

Marlin Glenfield Model 989G
Basically same as the Marlin Model
989 except: plain stock
Estimated Value: $75.00 - $95.00

Marlin

Marlin Model 70P Papoose

Marlin Model 70P Papoose
Caliber: 22 long rifle
Action: Semi-automatic; side ejection
Magazine: 7-shot clip
Barrel: 16¼"; quick takedown
Stock & Forearm: Smooth walnut-finish hardwood, semi-pistol grip one piece stock with abbreviated forearm; a takedown rifle with built-in flotation
Estimated Value: $110.00 - $135.00

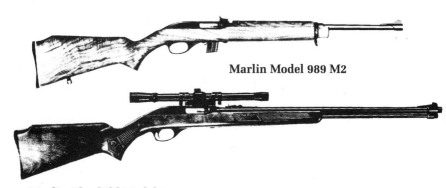

Marlin Model 989 M2

Marlin Glenfield Model 60

Marlin Model 99 M1
Caliber: 22 long rifle
Action: Semi-automatic; side ejection
Magazine: 9-shot tubular
Barrel: 18"; blued; micro-groove
Stock & Forearm: Carbine stock, hand guard, & barrel band; swivels
Estimated Value: $80.00 - $105.00

Marlin Model 60
Caliber: 22 long rifle
Action: Semi-automatic; side ejection
Magazine: 17-shot tubular, under barrel; reduced to 14-shot in 1992
Barrel: 22"; blued, round
Stock & Forearm: Checkered or smooth hardwood semi-pistol grip one piece stock & forearm, or Monte Carlo stock
Estimated Value: $90.00 - $110.00

Marlin Model 989 M2
Same as the Model 99 M1 except: 7-shot clip magazine
Estimated Value: $75.00 - $100.00

Marlin Model 75C
Same as the Model 60 except: 13-shot magazine; 18" barrel
Estimated Value: $80.00 - $100.00

Marlin Model 49

Marlin Model 49
Caliber: 22 long rifle
Action: Semi-automatic; side ejection
Magazine: 18-shot tubular
Barrel: 22"; blued, round
Stock & Forearm: Monte Carlo pistol grip stock
Estimated Value: $75.00 - $95.00

Marlin Model 49 DL
Same as the Model 49 except: checkered stock & forearm; gold-plated trigger
Estimated Value: $80.00 - $100.00

Marlin Model 70

Marlin Model 9 Camp Carbine

Marlin Model 9 & 9N Camp Carbine
Caliber: 9mm
Action: Semi-automatic; manual bolt hold-open, automatic last-shot bolt hold-open; side ejection
Magazine: 12-shot clip; 20-shot clip optional
Barrel: 16½"; round, blued, or nickel plate (9N); add 13% for nickel plate
Stock & Forearm: Walnut finished hardwood pistol grip one piece stock & forearm; rubber butt pad
Estimated Value: $215.00 - $275.00

Marlin Model 45
Similar to the Model 9 except: 45ACP caliber; 7-shot clip
Estimated Value: $215.00 - $275.00

Marlin Model 70 Carbine & 70HC
Caliber: 22 long rifle
Action: Semi-automatic; side ejection
Magazine: 7-shot clip; 70HC has 5, 15, or 25-shot clip
Barrel: 18"; blued, round
Stock & Forearm: Walnut Monte Carlo one piece plain stock & forearm; barrel band; swivels
Estimated Value: $100.00 - $124.00

Marlin Glenfield Model 40
Caliber: 22 long rifle
Action: Semi-auto; hammerless; side ejection
Magazine: 18-shot tubular
Barrel: 22"
Stock & Forearm: Checkered hardwood Monte Carlo semi-pistol grip stock & forearm
Estimated Value: $70.00 - $90.00

Marlin Model 990

Marlin Model 990L
Caliber: 22 long rifle
Action: Semi-automatic; last-shot bolt hold-open
Magazine: 14-shot tubular
Barrel: 22"; round with Miocrogroove rifling
Stock & Forearm: Laminated hardwood Monte Carlo one-piece pistol grip stock & forearm
Estimated Value: $130.00 - $160.00

Marlin Model 990
Caliber: 22 long rifle
Action: Semi-automatic; side ejection
Magazine: 18-shot tubular
Barrel: 22"; round
Stock & Forearm: Checkered walnut Monte Carlo one-piece pistol grip stock & forearm
Estimated Value: $105.00 - $130.00

Marlin Model 995
Similar to the Model 990 except: 7-shot clip magazine; 18" barrel
Estimated Value: $115.00 - $145.00

Mauser

Mauser Type B

Mauser Type A Special British
Caliber: 30-06, 7x57, 8x60, 9x57, or 9.3x62mm
Action: Bolt action; repeating
Magazine: 5-shot box
Barrel: 23½"; blued; octagon or round
Stock & Forearm: Checkered walnut one-piece pistol grip stock & tapered forearm; swivels
Estimated Value: $500.00 - $625.00

Mauser Type A Short Model
Similar to Type A Special British except: 21½" barrel & short action
Estimated Value: $480.00 - $625.00

Mauser Type A Magnum
Similar to Type A Special British except: magnum action for 280 Ross, 318 Express, 10.75x68mm, or 404 Express
Estimated Value: $540.00 - $700.00

Mauser Type B
Caliber: 30-06, 7x57, 8x57, 8x60, 9.3x62, or 10.75x68
Action: Bolt action; repeating
Magazine: 5-shot box
Barrel: 23½"; blued
Stock & Forearm: Checkered walnut one-piece pistol grip stock & lipped forearm; swivels
Estimated Value: $540.00 - $675.00

Mauser Type K
Similar to Type B except: 21½" barrel & short action
Estimated Value: $450.00 - $600.00

Mauser Model 98

Mauser Model MS 350B
Caliber: 22 long rifle
Action: Bolt action; repeating
Magazine: 5-shot box
Barrel: 27½"; blued
Stock & Forearm: Match-type, checkered pistol grip; swivels
Estimated Value: $375.00 - $500.00

Mauser Model 98
Caliber: 7mm or 7.9mm
Action: Bolt action; repeating
Magazine: 5-shot box
Barrel: 23½"; blued
Stock & Forearm: Walnut one-piece semi-pistol grip stock & fluted forearm; barrel band
Estimated Value: $450.00 - $575.00

Mauser Model ES 350
Similar to MS 350B except: Single shot; 26¾" barrel
Estimated Value: $340.00 - $450.00

Mauser Model ES 350B
Similar to MS 350B except: Single shot; Target sights
Estimated Value: $300.00 - $400.00

Mauser Type M
Caliber: 30-06, 6.5x54, 7x57, 8x52, 8x60, or 9x57
Action: Bolt action; repeating
Magazine: 5-shot box
Barrel: 19¾"; blued
Stock & Forearm: Checkered walnut one-piece pistol grip stock & full-length forearm; swivels
Estimated Value: $490.00 - $650.00

Mauser Model ES 340
Caliber: 22 long rifle
Action: Bolt action; Single shot
Magazine: None; single shot
Barrel: 25½"; blued
Stock & Forearm: Checkered walnut one-piece pistol grip stock & forearm; swivels
Estimated Value: $225.00 - $300.00

Mauser Type S
Caliber: 6.5x54, 7x57, 8x51, 8x60, or 9x57
Action: Bolt action; repeating
Magazine: 5-shot box
Barrel: 19¾"; blued
Stock & Forearm: Checkered walnut one-piece pistol grip stock & lipped full-length forearm; swivels
Estimated Value: $520.00 - $650.00

Mauser Model ES 340B
Similar to the ES 340 except: 26¾" barrel
Estimated Value: $240.00 - $320.00

Mauser Model EL 320
Similar to ES 340 except: 23½" barrel; adjustable rear sight
Estimated Value: $250.00 - $330.00

Mauser

Mauser Model MS 420

Mauser Model MS 420B
Similar to MS 420 except: better wood and finish
Estimated Value: $340.00 - $450.00

Mauser Model MS 420
Caliber: 22 long rifle
Action: Bolt action; repeating
Magazine: 5-shot detachable box
Barrel: 25½"; blued
Stock & Forearm: Checkered walnut one-piece pistol grip stock & forearm; swivels
Estimated Value: $300.00 - $380.00

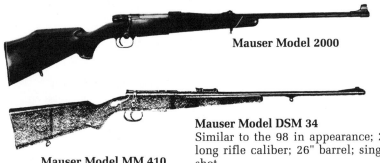

Mauser Model 2000

Mauser Model MM 410

Mauser Model DSM 34
Similar to the 98 in appearance; 22 long rifle caliber; 26" barrel; single shot
Estimated Value: $320.00 - $425.00

Mauser Model MM 410
Caliber: 22 long rifle
Action: Bolt action; repeating
Magazine: 5-shot detachable box
Barrel: 23½"; blued
Stock & Forearm: Checkered one-piece pistol grip stock & forearm; swivels
Estimated Value: $285.00 - $360.00

Mauser Model KKW
Similar to DSM 34; made from the mid to late 1930's
Estimated Value: $300.00 - $400.00

Mauser Model 2000
Caliber: 270 Win.; 308 Win.; 30-06
Action: Bolt action; repeating; adjustable trigger
Magazine: 5-shot box; hinged floor plate
Barrel: 24"; Krupp steel
Stock & Forearm: Checkered walnut Monte Carlo one-piece pistol grip stock & forearm; swivels
Estimated Value: $260.00 - $350.00

Mauser Model MM 410 B
Similar to MM 410 except: lighter weight
Estimated Value: $300.00 - $400.00

Mauser 3000

Mauser Model 3000
Caliber: 243, 270, 30-06, 308, 375 H&H mag., 7mm mag., or 300 Win. mag.
Action: Bolt action; repeating
Magazine: 5-shot box
Barrel: 22"; 26" in magnum; add $50.00 for mag.
Stock & Forearm: Checkered walnut Monte Carlo one-piece pistol grip stock & forearm; recoil pad; swivels
Estimated Value: $400.00 - $500.00

Mauser Model 660
Caliber: 243, 25-06, 270, 308, 30-06, 7x57, or 7mm
Action: Short bolt action; repeating
Magazine: 5-shot box
Barrel: 24"; blued
Stock & Forearm: Checkered walnut Monte Carlo one-piece pistol grip stock & forearm; swivels; recoil pad
Estimated Value: $490.00 - $650.00

Mauser Model 660 Safari
Similar to 660 except: magnum calibers in 458 Win., 375 H&H, 338 Win., or 7mm Rem.; 28" barrel; express rear sight
Estimated Value: $525.00 - $700.00

Mauser 660 Safari

Mauser Model 66S
Caliber: 243, 6.5x57, 270, 7x64, 30-06, 308, 5.6x61 V.H. mag., 6.5x68 mag., 7mm Rem. mag., 7mm V.H. mag., 8x68S mag., 300 Win. mag., 300 Weath. mag., 9.3x62 mag., or 9.3x64 mag.
Action: Mauser telescopic short bolt action; repeating
Magazine: 5-shot box
Barrel: 21", 24", or 26" (add $100.00 for 26" barrel); blued
Stock & Forearm: Select European walnut, checkered Monte Carlo one-piece pistol grip stock & forearm; rosewood tip on fore-end & pistol grip; recoil pad; swivels; full-length forearm optional (add $100.00)
Estimated Value: $800.00 - $1,000.00

Mauser Model 66SL
Similar to the Model 66SM except: select walnut stock & forearm; add $1,000.00 for Diplomat Model with custom engraving
Estimated Value: $1,025.00 - $1,370.00

Mauser Model 66SM
Similar to the Model 66S except: lipped forearm (no rosewood tip) & internal alterations; add $100.00 for 26" barrel or full-length forearm
Estimated Value: $870.00 - $1,160.00

Mauser Model 66S Big Game
Similar to Model 66S except: 375 H&H or 458 Win. magnum caliber; 26" barrel; fold down rear sight
Estimated Value: $1,050.00 - $1,320.00

Mauser Varminter 10

Mauser Model 77
Caliber: 243 Win., 270 Win., 308 Win., 30-06, 6.5x57, 7x64, 7mm Rem. mag., 6.5x68 mag., 300 Win. mag., 9.3x62 mag., or 8x68S mag.
Action: Mauser short bolt action; repeating
Magazine: 3-shot clip
Barrel: 20", 24", or 26"; blued
Stock & Forearm: Checkered walnut one-piece pistol grip stock & lipped forearm; full-length forearm optnal; recoil pad; swivels; add $100.00 for 26" barrel or full-length forearm
Estimated Value: $685.00 - $915.00

Mauser Model 77 DJV Sportsman
Similar to the Model 77 except: stippled stock & forearm
Estimated Value: $860.00 - $1,150.00

Mauser Model 77 Big Game
Similar to the Model 77 except: 375 H&H magnum caliber; 26" barrel
Estimated Value: $800.00 - $1,070.00

Mauser Varminter 10
Caliber: 22-250
Action: Bolt action; repeating
Magazine: 5-shot box
Barrel: 24", heavy; blued
Stock & Forearm: Checkered walnut Monte Carlo one-piece pistol grip stock & forearm
Estimated Value: $350.00 - $440.00

Mossberg

Mossberg Model M
Caliber: 22 short, long, or long rifle
Action: Bolt action; cocking piece
Magazine: None; single shot
Barrel: 20"; round; blued
Stock & Forearm: Plain one-piece semi-pistol grip stock & tapered forearm; a boys' rifle made in the early 1930's
Estimated Value: $55.00 - $70.00

Mossberg Model R
Caliber: 22 short, long, or long rifle
Action: Bolt action; repeating
Magazine: Tubular; 14 long rifles, 16 longs, or 20 shorts
Barrel: 24"; blued
Stock & Forearm: Walnut semi-pistol grip stock & forearm
Estimated Value: $60.00 - $80.00

Mossberg Model B
Caliber: 22 short, long, or long rifle
Action: Bolt action
Magazine: None; single shot
Barrel: 22"; blued
Stock & Forearm: Plain wood semi-pistol grip stock & forearm
Estimated Value: $60.00 - $75.00

Mossberg Model 35

Mossberg Model 14
Caliber: 22 short, long, or long rifle
Action: Bolt action
Magazine: None; single shot
Barrel: 24"; blued
Stock & Forearm: Plain one-piece semi-pistol grip stock & forearm; swivels
Estimated Value: $55.00 - $70.00

Mossberg Model 10
Caliber: 22 short, long, or long rifle
Action: Bolt action
Magazine: None; single shot
Barrel: 22"; blued
Stock & Forearm: Walnut semi-pistol grip stock & forearm; swivels
Estimated Value: $60.00 - $75.00

Mossberg Model 20
Similar to the Model 10 except: 24" barrel & grooved forearm
Estimated Value: $55.00 - $70.00

Mossberg Model 30
Similar to the Model 20 with peep rear sight & hooded ramp front sight
Estimated Value: $60.00 - $75.00

Mossberg Model 40
Similar to the Model 30 except: bolt action; repeating; tubular magazine that holds 16 long rifles, 18 longs, 22 shorts
Estimated Value: $70.00 - $90.00

Mossberg Model 34
Similar to the Model 14, made in the mid 1930's
Estimated Value: $65.00 - $80.00

Mossberg Model 35
Caliber: 22 short, long, or long rifle
Action: Bolt action
Magazine: None; single shot
Barrel: 26"; blued; heavy
Stock & Forearm: Plain walnut one-piece semi-pistol grip stock & forearm; cheekpiece; swivels
Estimated Value: $100.00 - $125.00

Mossberg Model 35A
Similar to the Model 35 except: target stock & sights
Estimated Value: $105.00 - $130.00

Mossberg Model 35A-LS
Similar to the Model 35A with special Lyman sights
Estimated Value: $105.00 - $130.00

Mossberg

Mossberg Model 26B

Mossberg Model 25
Caliber: 22 short, long, or long rifle
Action: Bolt action
Magazine: None; single shot
Barrel: 24"; blued
Stock & Forearm: Plain walnut one-piece pistol grip stock & forearm; swivels
Estimated Value: $50.00 - $65.00

Mossberg Model 26B
Caliber: 22 short, long, or long rifle
Action: Bolt action
Magazine: None; single shot
Barrel: 26"; blued
Stock & Forearm: Plain one-piece semi-pistol grip stock & forearm; swivels
Estimated Value: $55.00 - $75.00

Mossberg Model 25A
Similar to the Model 25 except: higher quality finish & better wood
Estimated Value: $55.00 - $70.00

Mossberg Model 26C
Similar to the 26B without swivels or peep sight
Estimated Value: $50.00 - $65.00

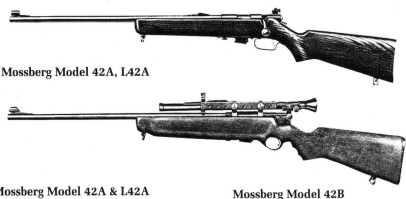

Mossberg Model 42A, L42A

Mossberg Model 42B

Mossberg Model 42A & L42A
Similar to the Model 42 except: higher quality; L42A is left hand action
Estimated Value: $65.00 - $80.00

Mossberg Model 42B
An improved version of the Model 42A with micrometer peep sight & 5-shot magazine; made from the late 1930's to early 1940's
Estimated Value: $65.00 - $85.00

Mossberg Model 42
Caliber: 22 short, long, or long rifle
Action: Bolt action; repeating
Magazine: 7-shot detachable
Barrel: 24"; blued
Stock & Forearm: Plain walnut one-piece semi-pistol grip stock & forearm; swivels; takedown model
Estimated Value: $60.00 - $75.00

Mossberg Model 42C

Mossberg Model 42C
Similar to the Model 42B without the peep sight
Estimated Value: $65.00 - $80.00

Mossberg Model 42M
Newer version of the Model 42 with a 23" barrel; full-length forearm; cheekpiece
Estimated Value: $70.00 - $85.00

Mossberg Model 42MB
Similar to the Model 42; used as military training rifle in Great Britain in World War II; full stock
Estimated Value: $125.00 - $160.00

Mossberg Model 43 & L43
Caliber: 22 long rifle
Action: Bolt action; repeating
Magazine: 7-shot detachable box
Barrel: 26"; blued
Stock & Forearm: Walnut one-piece semi-pistol grip stock & forearm; cheekpiece; swivels. L43 is left hand action
Estimated Value: $85.00 - $110.00

Mossberg Model 44
Caliber: 22 short, long, or long rifle
Action: Bolt action; repeating
Magazine: Tubular; 16 long rifles, 18 longs, 22 shorts
Barrel: 24"; blued
Stock & Forearm: Plain walnut one-piece semi-pistol grip stock & forearm; swivels
Estimated Value: $70.00 - $85.00

Mossberg Model 43B

Mossberg Model 43B
Similar to the Model 44B except: special Lyman sights
Estimated Value: $110.00 - $135.00

Mossberg Model 44 U.S.
Improved version of the Model 44B; made in the early 1930's to late 1940's; used as a training rifle for U.S. armed forces in World War II
Estimated Value: $105.00 - $130.00

Mossberg Model 44B
Caliber: 22 long rifle
Action: Bolt action; repeating
Magazine: 7-shot detachable box
Barrel: 26"; heavy barrel
Stock & Forearm: Plain one-piece semi-pistol grip stock & forearm; swivels; cheekpiece
Estimated Value: $100.00 - $125.00

Mossberg Model 35B
Single shot version of the Model 44B; made in the late 1930's
Estimated Value: $90.00 - $115.00

Mossberg

Mossberg Model 45

Mossberg Model 45A, L45A

Mossberg Model 45B

Mossberg Model 46

Mossberg Model 45
Caliber: 22 short, long, or long rifle
Action: Bolt action; repeating
Magazine: Tubular; 15 long rifles, 18
longs, 22 shorts
Barrel: 24"; blued
Stock & Forearm: Plain one-piece
semi-pistol grip stock & forearm;
swivels
Estimated Value: $60.00 - $75.00

Mossberg Model 45C
Similar to the Model 45 without
sights
Estimated Value: $55.00 - $70.00

Mossberg Model 45A & L45A
Improved version of the Model 45,
made in the late 1930's; L45A is left
hand action
Estimated Value: $65.00 - $80.00

Mossberg Model 45AC
Similar to the Model 45A without
sights
Estimated Value: $55.00 - $70.00

Mossberg Model 45B
Similar to the Model 45A with open
rear sight; made in the late 1930's
Estimated Value: $65.00 - $80.00

Mossberg Model 46
Caliber: 22 short, long, or long rifle
Action: Bolt action; repeating
Magazine: Tubular; 15 long rifles, 18
longs, 22 shorts
Barrel: 26"; blued
Stock & Forearm: Plain one-piece
semi-piece grip stock & forearm;
cheekpiece; swivels
Estimated Value: $60.00 - $80.00

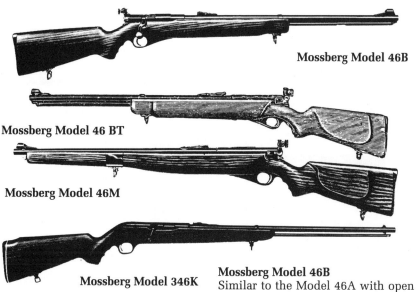

Mossberg Model 46B

Mossberg Model 46 BT

Mossberg Model 46M

Mossberg Model 346K

Mossberg Model 46C
A heavy barrel version of the Model 46
Estimated Value: $65.00 - $85.00

Mossberg Model 46A
An improved version of the Model 46 made in the late 1930's
Estimated Value: $60.00 - $85.00

Mossberg Model 46AC
Similar to the 46A with open rear sight
Estimated Value: $60.00 - $75.00

Mossberg Model 46A-LS & L46A-LS
Similar to the Model 46A with special Lyman sights; L46A-LS is left hand action
Estimated Value: $75.00 - $95.00

Mossberg Model 46B
Similar to the Model 46A with open rear sight and receiver peep sight; made in the late 1930's
Estimated Value: $60.00 - $80.00

Mossberg Model 46BT
A heavy barrel version of the Model 46B
Estimated Value: $70.00 - $95.00

Mossberg Model 46M
Similar to the Model 46 with full-length two-piece forearm; made about 1940 to the early 1950's
Estimated Value: $65.00 - $90.00

Mossberg Model 346K & 346B
Caliber: 22 short, long, or long rifle
Action: Bolt action; repeating
Magazine: Tubular; 20 long rifles, 23 longs, 30 shorts
Barrel: 26"; blued
Stock & Forearm: Plain Monte Carlo one-piece pistol grip stock & lipped forearm; swivels; model 346B has peep sights.
Estimated Value: $60.00 - $85.00

Mossberg

Mossberg Model 346B

Mossberg Model 320K

Mossberg Model 340B

Mossberg Model 320B

Mossberg Model 340M Carbine

Mossberg Model 342K

Mossberg Model 320K
Single shot version of the Model 346K
Estimated Value: $60.00 - $75.00

Mossberg Model 340K
Similar to the Model 346K except: 7-shot clip
Estimated Value: $60.00 - $80.00

Mossberg Model 340B
Similar to the 346B except: 7-shot clip
Estimated Value: $60.00 - $75.00

Mossberg Model 342K
Similar to the 340K except: 18" barrel; hinged forearm; side mounted swivels
Estimated Value: $60.00 - $75.00

Mossberg Model 320B
Similar to the 340K except: single shot; auto safety
Estimated Value: $60.00 - $80.00

Mossberg Model 340M Carbine
Similar to the Model 340K with full-length forearm & 18" barrel
Estimated Value: $65.00 - $90.00

Mossberg Model 146B

Mossberg Model 144

Mossberg Model 144
Caliber: 22 long rifle
Action: Bolt action; repeating
Magazine: 7-shot clip
Barrel: 26"; heavy; blued
Stock & Forearm: Walnut one-piece semi-pistol grip stock & forearm; hand rest; swivels
Estimated Value: $135.00 - $180.00

Mossberg Model 146B
Caliber: 22 short, long, or long rifle
Action: Bolt action; repeating
Magazine: Tubular; 20 long rifles, 23 longs, or 30 shorts
Barrel: 26"; blued
Stock & Forearm: Plain Monte Carlo one-piece pistol grip stock & lipped forearm; swivels
Estimated Value: $70.00 - 90.00

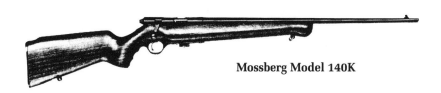

Mossberg Model 140K

Mossberg Model 140B

Mossberg Model 140B
Similar to the 140K except: hooded ramp front sight & peep rear sight
Estimated Value: $70.00 - $85.00

Mossberg Model 140K
Caliber: 22 short, long, or long rifle
Action: Bolt action; repeating
Magazine: 7-shot clip
Barrel: 26½"; blued
Stock & Forearm: Walnut Monte Carlo one-piece pistol grip stock & forearm; ; swivels
Estimated Value: $65.00 - $80.00

Mossberg

Mossberg Model 640K

Mossberg Model 620K

Mossberg Model 321K

Mossberg Model 341

Mossberg Model 640K
Caliber: 22 magnum
Action: Bolt action; repeating
Magazine: 5-shot box
Barrel: 24"; blued
Stock & Forearm: Checkered walnut Monte Carlo one-piece pistol grip stock & forearm; swivels
Estimated Value: $80.00 - $110.00

Mossberg Model 620K
Similar to the 640K except: single shot
Estimated Value: $60.00 - $75.00

Mossberg Model 321K
Caliber: 22 short, long, or long rifle
Action: Bolt action
Magazine: None; single shot
Barrel: 24"; blued
Stock & Forearm: Checkered Monte Carlo one-piece pistol grip stock & forearm
Estimated Value: $55.00 - $70.00

Mossberg Model 341
Similar to the 321K except: 7-shot clip magazine; bolt action repeater; swivels
Estimated Value: $60.00 - $80.00

Mossberg Model 800A

Mossberg Model 800 Varmint

Mossberg Model 810

Mossberg Model 800A
Caliber: 308, 243, 22-250, or 222
Rem.
Action: Bolt action; repeating
Magazine: 4-shot box
Barrel: 22"; blued
Stock & Forearm: Checkered wood
Monte Carlo one-piece pistol grip
stock & forearm; swivels
Estimated Value: $150.00 - $200.00

Mossberg Model 800 Varmint
Similar to the Model 800A except:
24" barrel with scope mounts; in 243
or 22-250 calibers only
Estimated Value: $180.00 - $225.00

Mossberg Model 800 Target
Similar to the Model 800A except:
scope mounts and scope in 308, 243,
or 22-250 calibers
Estimated Value: $190.00 - $250.00

Mossberg Model 810
Caliber: 30-06, 7mm Rem. mag., or
270 Win.
Action: Bolt action; repeating
Magazine: 4-shot detachable box
Barrel: 22"; blued
Stock & Forearm: Checkered Monte
Carlo one-piece pistol grip stock &
forearm; swivels; recoil pad; add
$15.00 for 7mm Rem. magnum
Estimated Value: $165.00 - $220.00

Mossberg Model RM-7A
Caliber: 30-06
Action: Bolt action; repeating;
hammerless
Magazine: 4-shot rotary
Barrel: 22"; round
Stock & Forearm: Checkered walnut
one-piece pistol grip stock &
forearm; fluted comb; recoil pad
Estimated Value: $160.00 - $215.00

Mossberg Model RM-7B
Similar to the Model RM-7A except:
7mm Rem. magnum caliber; 3-shot
magazine; 24" barrel
Estimated Value: $170.00 - $225.00

Mossberg

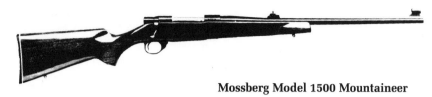

Mossberg Model 1500 Mountaineer

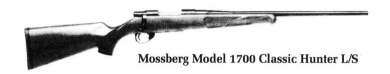

Mossberg Model 1700 Classic Hunter L/S

Mossberg Model 1500 Varmint

Mossberg Model 1500 Varmint
Similar to the Model 1500 except: 24" heavy barrel in 223, 22-250 or 308 caliber; Monte Carlo stock; blued or parkerized finish
Estimated Value: $240.00 - $320.00

Mossberg Model 1500 Mountaineer
Caliber: 223, 22-250, 243, 270, 308, 30-06, 7mm magnum, 300 Win. magnum, or 338 Win. magnum
Action: Bolt action, hammerless; repeating
Magazine: 5 or 6-shot box
Barrel: 22" or 24"
Stock & Forearm: Checkered walnut one-piece pistol grip stock & forearm; recoil pad on magnum; add $15.00 for magnum & $20.00 for sights
Estimated Value: $190.00 - $255.00

Mossberg Model 1550 Mountaineer
Similar to the Model 1500 except: removable magazine; 22" barrel; 243, 270, or 30-06 calibers; add $20.00 for sights
Estimated Value: $200.00 - $270.00

Mossberg Model 1700 Classic Hunter L/S
Similar to the Model 1500 except: 22" barrel; removable magazine; lipped forearm; pistol grip cap & recoil pad; calibers: 243, 270, or 30-06
Estimated Value: $255.00 - $340.00

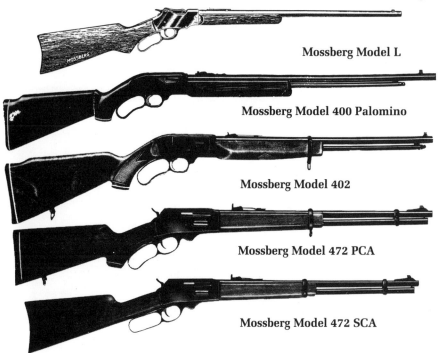

Mossberg Model L

Mossberg Model 400 Palomino

Mossberg Model 402

Mossberg Model 472 PCA

Mossberg Model 472 SCA

Mossberg Model L
Caliber: 22 short, long, or long rifle
Action: Lever-action, falling block
Magazine: None; single shot
Barrel: 24"; blued
Stock & Forearm: Plain walnut semi-pistol grip stock & small forearm; made from the late 1920's to early 1930's
Estimated Value: $220.00 - $275.00

Mossberg Model 400 Palomino
Caliber: 22 short, long, or long rifle
Action: Lever-action, hammerless; repeating
Magazine: Tubular; 15 long rifles, 17 longs, or 20 shorts
Barrel: 24"; blued
Stock & Forearm: Checkered walnut Monte Carlo pistol grip stock & forearm; barrel bands; swivels
Estimated Value: $80.00 - $100.00

Mossberg Model 402
Similar to the Model 400 Palomino except: shorter barrel; smaller magazine capacity; checkering on stock and forearm
Estimated Value: $70.00 - $90.00

Mossberg Model 472 PCA, SCA, 479 PCA, SCA
Caliber: 30-30 or 35 Rem.
Action: Lever-action; exposed hammer; repeating
Magazine: 6-shot tubular
Barrel: 20"; blued
Stock & Forearm: Plain pistol grip stock & forearm; barrel band; swivels; or straight grip stock (SCA); sold first as the 472 Series, then as the 479 Series
Estimated Value: $130.00 - $165.00

Mossberg

Mossberg Model 472 PRA

Mossberg Model 479

Mossberg Model 472 Brush Gun
Similar to the Model 472 PCA
except: 18" barrel; straight stock; 5-
shot magazine
Estimated Value: $145.00 - $180.00

Mossberg Model 472 PRA, SBA
Similar to the Model 472 PCA, SCA
except: 24" barrel; hooded front sight
Estimated Value: $135.00 - $170.00

Mossberg Model 479
Caliber: 30-30 Win.
Action: Lever action, exposed
hammer, repeating
Magazine: 5-shot tubular
Barrel: 20"
Stock & Forearm: Hardwood semi-
pistol grip stock and forearm; barrel
band
Estimated Value: $150.00 - $200.00

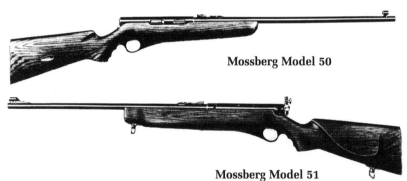

Mossberg Model 50

Mossberg Model 51

Mossberg Model K
Caliber: 22 short, long, or long rifle
Action: Slide action; hammerless;
repeating
Magazine: Tubular; 14 long rifles, 16
longs, or 20 shorts
Barrel: 22"; blued
Stock & Forearm: Plain walnut
straight grip stock & grooved slide
handle
Estimated Value: $130.00 - $165.00

Mossberg Model 50 & 51
Caliber: 22 long rifle
Action: Semi-automatic; hammerless
Magazine: 15-shot tubular (in stock)
Barrel: 24"; blued
Stock & Forearm: Walnut one-piece
semi-pistol grip stock & forearm;
swivels on Model 51
Estimated Value: $75.00 - $90.00

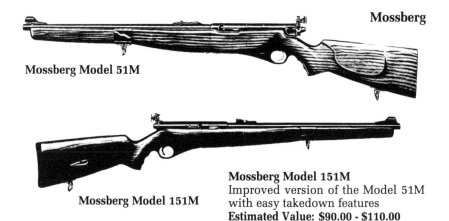

Mossberg

Mossberg Model 51M

Mossberg Model 151M

Mossberg Model 151M
Improved version of the Model 51M with easy takedown features
Estimated Value: $90.00 - $110.00

Mossberg Model 51M
Similar to the Model 51 except: full-length, two-piece forearm; 20" barrel
Estimated Value: $80.00 - $100.00

Mossberg Model 151K
Similar to the 151M except: Monte Carlo stock; standard length lipped forearm; 24" barrel; no swivels
Estimated Value: $95.00 - $115.00

Mossberg Model 152

Mossberg Model 142

Mossberg Model 152K
Similar to the Model 152 except: open rear sight; shorter barrel
Estimated Value: $75.00 - $95.00

Mossberg Model 152
Caliber: 22 long rifle
Action: Semi-automatic
Magazine: 7-shot detachable box
Barrel: 18"; blued
Stock & Forearm: Plain one-piece semi-pistol grip stock & hinged forearm (for forward grip); side mounted swivels
Estimated Value: $85.00 - $110.00

Mossberg Model 142
Similar to the Model 152 except: bolt action; in short, long, or long rifle; peep sight
Estimated Value: $70.00 - $90.00

Mossberg Model 142K
Similar to the Model 142 except: open rear sight
Estimated Value: $65.00 - $80.00

Pocket Guide to Rifles

87

Mossberg

Mossberg Model 430

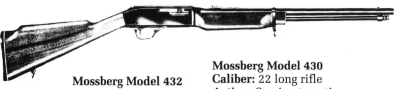

Mossberg Model 432

Mossberg Model 432
Similar to the Model 430 except: straight grip stock; barrel band; smaller capacity magazine
Estimated Value: $70.00 - $85.00

Mossberg Model 430
Caliber: 22 long rifle
Action: Semi-automatic
Magazine: 18-shot tubular
Barrel: 24"; blued
Stock & Forearm: Checkered walnut Monte Carlo pistol grip stock & forearm
Estimated Value: $75.00 - $90.00

Mossberg Model 350K

Mossberg Model 351 C (Carbine)

Mossberg Model 351K

Mossberg Model 351 C (Carbine)
Similar to the 351K except: 18½" barrel; barrel bands; swivels
Estimated Value: $65.00 - $80.00

Mossberg Model 351K
Caliber: 22 long rifle
Action: Semi-automatic
Magazine: 15-shot tubular (in stock)
Barrel: 24"; blued
Stock & Forearm: Walnut Monte Carlo one-piece semi-pistol grip stock and forearm
Estimated Value: $70.00 - $85.00

Mossberg Model 350K
Caliber: 22 long rifle
Action: Semi-automatic
Magazine: 7-shot clip
Barrel: 23½"; blued
Stock & Forearm: Walnut Monte Carlo one-piece semi-pistol grip stock & forearm
Estimated Value: $70.00 - $90.00

Mossberg Model 377 Plinkster

Mossberg Model 352K Carbine

Mossberg Model 352K Carbine
Caliber: 22 long rifle
Action: Semi-automatic
Magazine: 7-shot clip
Barrel: 18½"; blued
Stock & Forearm: Walnut Monte Carlo one-piece semi-pistol grip stock & forearm; swivels; hinged forearm (for forward grip)
Estimated Value: $70.00 - $90.00

Mossberg Model 377 Plinkster
Caliber: 22 long rifle
Action: Semi-automatic; hammerless
Magazine: 15-shot tubular (in stock)
Barrel: 20"; round
Stock & Forearm: Molded structural foam; one-piece Monte Carlo pistol grip stock & forearm; thumb hole in stock
Estimated Value: $65.00 - $85.00

Mossberg Model 353
Similar to the 352K except: 18" barrel, adjustable sight
Estimated Value: $70.00 - $90.00

Musketeer

Musketeer Mauser

Musketeer Mauser
Caliber: 243, 25-06, 270, 264 mag., 308, 30-06, 7mm mag., or 300 mag.
Action: FN Mauser bolt action
Magazine: 5-shot; 3-shot in magnum
Barrel: 24"; blued
Stock & Forearm: Checkered walnut Monte Carlo one-piece pistol grip stock & forearm
Estimated Value: $225.00 - $300.00

Musketeer Carbine
Same as Musketeer Mauser except: shorter barrel
Estimated Value: $210.00 - $275.00

New England

New England Handi-Gun Combination

Same as the Handi-Rifle except any combination of rifle or shotgun barrels are available to be used interchangeably. Shotgun barrels have brass bead front sight with blued or nickel finish; add 10% for nickel; 22" barrel in 12 or 20 gauge; prices are for rifle & shotgun barrel combinations
Estimated Value: $170.00 - $215.00

New England Handi-Rifle

Caliber: 223 Rem., 22 Hornet, 30-30 Win., 243 Win., 30-06, or 45-70 Gov't
Action: Break open; side release lever; exposed hammer
Magazine: None; single shot
Barrel: 22"; blued
Stock & Forearm: Hardwood, walnut finish, pistol grip, smooth stock & semi-beavertail forearm; swivels
Estimated Value: $120.00 - $155.00

New Haven

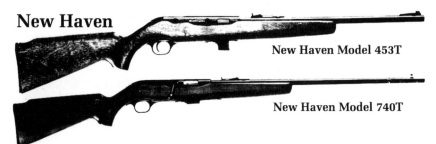

New Haven Model 453T

New Haven Model 740T

New Haven Model 679

Caliber: 30-30 Win.
Action: Lever-action; exposed hammer; repeating
Magazine: 5-shot tubular
Barrel: 20"; blued
Stock & Forearm: Plain birch semi-pistol grip stock & forearm; barrel band
Estimated Value: $130.00 - $160.00

New Haven Model 740T

Caliber: 22 Win. mag.
Action: Bolt action; hammerless; repeating
Magazine: 5-shot clip
Barrel: 26"; blued
Stock & Forearm: Plain birch one-piece Monte Carlo pistol grip stock & forearm
Estimated Value: $65.00 - $85.00

New Haven Model 740TS

Similar to the Model 740T except: 4X scope
Estimated Value: $65.00 - $90.00

New Haven Model 453T

Caliber: 22 short, long, or long rifle
Action: Semi-automatic; hammerless
Magazine: 7-shot clip
Barrel: 18"; blued
Stock & Forearm: Plain one-piece Monte Carlo pistol grip stock & forearm
Estimated Value: $65.00 - $85.00

New Haven Model 453 TS

Similar to the Model 453T except: 4X scope
Estimated Value: $70.00 - $90.00

Newton

Newton Standard, 1st Model

Newton, Buffalo Newton

Newton Standard, 1st Model
Caliber: 22, 256, 280, 30-06, 30 Newton, or 35 Nev ton
Action: Bolt action; double set trigger
Magazine: 5-shot box
Barrel: 24"; blued
Stock & Forearm: Checkered wood pistol grip stock & lipped forearm; made for a short time before World War I
Estimated Value: $540.00 - $675.00

Newton Standard, 2nd Model
Similar to 1st Model except: improved action; made to about 1920's.
Estimated Value: $575.00 - $720.00

Newton, Buffalo Newton
Similar to the 2nd Model; made from the early 1920's to early 1930's
Estimated Value: $470.00 - $625.00

Newton Mauser
Caliber: 256
Action: Mauser-type bolt action; reversed double set trigger
Magazine: 5-shot box
Barrel: 24"; blued
Stock & Forearm: Checkered wood pistol grip stock & lipped forearm; made in the early 1920's
Estimated Value: $480.00 - $600.00

Noble

Noble Model 33

Noble Model 33A
Similar to the Model 33 except: wood stock and slide handle; made until the mid 1950's
Estimated Value: $75.00 - $95.00

Noble Model 33
Caliber: 22 short, long, or long rifle
Action: Slide action; hammerless; repeating
Magazine: Tubular; 15 long rifles, 17 longs, or 21 shorts
Barrel: 24"; blued
Stock & Forearm: Semi-pistol grip tenite stock & groved slide handle; made from the late 1940's to early 1950's
Estimated Value: $70.00 - $90.00

Noble

Noble Model 10

Noble Model 222

Nobel Model 222
Caliber: 22 short, long, or long rifle
Action: Bolt action
Magazine: None; single shot
Barrel: 22"; blued
Stock & Forearm: Wood one-piece
semi-pistol grip stock & forearm
Estimated Value: $50.00 - $65.00

Noble Model 10
Caliber: 22 short, long, or long rifle
Action: Bolt action
Magazine: None; single shot
Barrel: 24"; blued
Stock & Forearm: Walnut one-piece
semi-pistol grip stock & forearm
Estimated Value: $55.00 - $65.00

Noble Model 20
Similar to the Model 10 except: 22"
barrel; slightly curved buttplate
Estimated Value: $60.00 - $70.00

Noble Model 235

Noble Model 835

Noble Model 835
Similar to the Model 235; made in
the early 1970's.
Estimated Value: $75.00 - $95.00

Noble Model 235
Caliber: 22 short, long, or long rifle
Action: Slide action; hammerless;
repeating
Magazine: Tubular; 15 long rifles, 17
longs, or 21 shorts
Barrel: 24"; blued
Stock & Forearm: Wood semi-pistol
grip stock & grooved slide handle
Estimated Value: $70.00 - $90.00

Noble Model 275

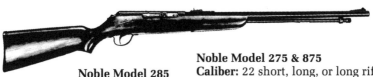

Noble Model 285

Noble Model 285 & 885
Caliber: 22 long rifle
Action: Semi-automatic
Magazine: 15-shot tubular
Barrel: 22"; blued
Stock & Forearm: Wood one-piece semi-pistol grip stock & forearm
Estimated Value: $75.00 - $95.00

Noble Model 275 & 875
Caliber: 22 short, long, or long rifle
Action: Lever-action; hammerless; repeating
Magazine: Tubular; 15 long rifles, 17 longs, or 21 shorts
Barrel: 24"; blued
Stock & Forearm: Wood one-piece semi-pistol grip stock & forearm; made from the late 1950's to early 1970's (Model 275); early to mid 1970's (Model 875)
Estimated Value: $85.00 - $110.00

Pedersen

Pedersen Model 3000

Pedersen Model 3000
Caliber: 270, 30-06, 7mm mag., or 338 Win mag.
Action: Bolt action; adjustable trigger
Magazine: 3-shot box
Barrel: 22" or 24"; blued
Stock & Forearm: Checkered walnut one-piece pistol grip stock & forearm; cheekpiece; swivels; made in three grades during the 1970's
Estimated Value:
  Grade I: $600.00 - $800.00
  Grade II: $500.00 - $620.00
  Grade III: $375.00 - $500.00

Pedersen/Plainfield

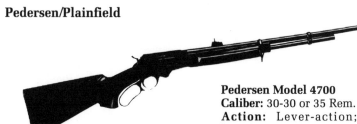

Pedersen Model 4700

Pedersen Model 4700
Caliber: 30-30 or 35 Rem.
Action: Lever-action; exposed hammer; repeating
Magazine: 5-shot tubular
Barrel: 24"; blued
Stock & Forearm: Walnut pistol grip stock & short forearm; barrel band; swivels
Estimated Value: $175.00 - $250.00

Plainfield

Plainfield Model M1

Plainfield Deluxe Sporter

Plainfield Commando

Plainfield Model M1 Sporter
Similar to the Model M1 except: wood hand guard; no slot in the stock (See Iver Johnson)
Estimated Value: $135.00 - $185.00

Plainfield Deluxe Sporter
or Plainfielder
Similar to the M-1 Sporter except: checkered walnut Monte Carlo pistol grip stock & forearm
Estimated Value: $130.00 - $175.00

Plainfield Model M1
Caliber: 30 M1 or 223 (5.7mm)
Action: Semi-auto, gas operated
Magazine: 15-shot detachable clip
Barrel: 18"; blued or stainless steel
Stock & Forearm: Wood one-piece semi-pistol grip stock & forearm; slot in stock (for sling); metal ventilated hand guard; made from about 1960 to late 1970's; reintroduced in the late 1970's by Iver Johnson (See Iver Johnson); add 30% for stainless steel
Estimated Value: $130.00 - $175.00

Plainfield Commando
or Paratrooper
Similar to the Model M1 except: pistol grip at rear; vertical hand grip on forearm; telescoping wire shoulder stock; add 30% for stainless steel (See Iver Johnson)
Estimated Value: $160.00 - $210.00

Pocket Guide to Rifles

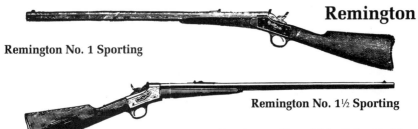

Remington

Remington No. 1 Sporting

Remington No. 1½ Sporting

Remington Military Breech-Loading
Caliber: C.F. 43 Spanish, 43 Egyptian, 50-70 Government, or 58 Berdan; early models used rim fire cartridges; models for center fire cartridges produced after 1872
Action: Single shot; rolling block with single trigger; visible hammer
Magazine: None; single shot
Barrel: 30" to 36"; round
Stock & Forearm: Plain walnut straight grip stock & long forearm with ram rod; steel buttplate; made from about 1867 to 1902 (large number sold to Egypt, France & Spain) & sold commercially in U.S.A.; some are unmarked; some have Arabic marked barrels & some marked Remington
Estimated Value: $130.00 - $175.00

Remington No. 1 Sporting
Caliber: Early guns for rim fire 50-70, 44 long & extra long or 46 long & extra long; after 1872 made for centerfire 40-50, 40-70, 44-77, 45-70, or 45 sporting cartridge
Action: Single shot; rolling block with single trigger; visible hammer
Magazine: None; single shot
Barrel: 28" or 30"; tapered octagon
Stock & Forearm: Plain walnut straight grip stock with flanged-top steel buttplate & short plain walnut forearm with thin round front; made from about 1868 to 1902
Estimated Value: $260.00 - $350.00

Remington No. 1 Light Baby Carbine
Caliber: 44-40
Action: Single-shot; rolling block with single trigger; visible hammer
Magazine: None; single shot
Barrel: 20"; light round
Stock & Forearm: Plain oiled walnut straight stock with metal buttplate & short forearm; barrel band
Estimated Value: $300.00 - $400.00

Remington No. 1½ Sporting
Similar to No. 1 Sporting Rifle except: lighter action, stocks & smaller calibers; made in following pistol calibers: rim fire 22 short, long or extra long; 25 Stevens or 25 long; 32 or 38 long & extra long; center fire Winchester 32-20, 38-40, or 44-40; barrel lengths 24", 26", 28", or 30"; made from about 1869 to 1902
Estimated Value: $225.00 - $300.00

Remington No. 2 Sporting
Caliber: Early models were for rim fire 22, 25, 32 or 38. Later models for center fire 22, 25-20, 25-25, 32 long, 38 long or 38-40
Action: Single-shot; rolling block; single trigger
Magazine: None; single shot
Barrel: 24" to 30"; lightweight; octagon
Stock & Forearm: Plain oil-finish walnut, straight grip stock & lipped forearm; made from about 1873 to 1902
Estimated Value: $240.00 - $325.00

Remington

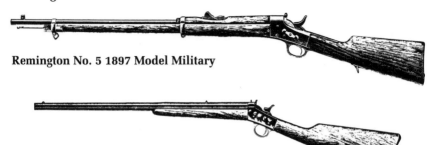

Remington No. 5 1897 Model Military

Remington No. 5 1897 Carbine
Caliber: 7mm
Action: Single shot; rolling block; ornance steel; smokeless powder action with case hardened steel frame; visible hammer
Magazine: None; single shot
Barrel: 20"; round barrel
Stock & Forearm: Plain straight grip, oiled walnut, two-piece stock & short forearm; steel buttplate; barrel band; hand guard; made from about 1897 to 1906.
Estimated Value: $270.00 - $340.00

Remington-Hepburn No. 3 Sporting
Caliber: Center fire 22, 25-20, 25-25, 32, 32-20, 32-30, 32-40, 38, 38-40, 38-50, 38-55, 40-60, 40-65, 40-80, 45-70 Government, or 45-90; also made by order for 40-50, 40-70, 40-90 or 44-70 bottle neck Remington, 45-90, 45-105, 50-90 Sharps, or 50-70 Government.
Action: Hepburn drop block; side-lever opens & closes action; single-shot with low visible hammer; early models with single trigger; later models with single or double set triggers
Magazine: None; single shot
Barrel: 28" to 32"; round, octagon, or half octagon
Stock & Forearm: Plain straight grip or checkered pistol grip, oiled wood stock with steel buttplate & matching short lipped forearm; made from about 1880 to 1906
Estimated Value: $560.00 - $700.00

Remington No. 4 New Model

Remington No. 5
1897 Model Military
Caliber: 7mm or 30 Government
Action: Single-shot; rolling block; smokeless powder action with case hardened frame; visible hammer
Magazine: None; single shot
Barrel: 30"; light round tapered barrel
Stock & Forearm: Plain straight grip, oiled walnut, two-piece stock with steel buttplate & full length capped forearm; two barrel bands; hand guard; made from about 1897 to 1906
Estimated Value: $225.00 - $300.00

Remington No. 4 New Model
Caliber: Rim fire only in 22 short, long or long rifle; 25 Stevens or 32 long
Action: Single-shot; rolling block; light short action with automatic shell ejector; visible hammer
Magazine: None; single shot
Barrel: 22½"; light octagon in 22 or 25 caliber; 24" in 32 caliber; round barrel after about 1931
Stock & Forearm: Plain varnished, two-piece straight grip stock & short round front forearm; made from about 1891 to 1934
Estimated Value: $185.00 - $230.00

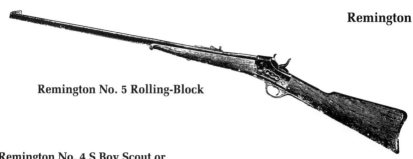

Remington No. 5 Rolling-Block

Remington No. 4 S Boy Scout or Military Model
Caliber: 22 short only until 1915; then chambered for 22 short or 22 long
Action: Case hardened No. 4 rolling-block action; visible hammer
Magazine: None; single-shot
Barrel: 28"; medium, round barrel
Stock & Forearm: Musket-style, oiled walnut, one-piece, stock & full-length forearm; steel buttplate & barrel band; bayonet lug; hand guard; called Boy Scout model from 1913 to 1915 then renamed Military Model
Estimated Value: $320.00 - $400.00

Remington No. 5 Rolling-Block
Caliber: 7mm Mauser, 30-30, or 30-40 Krag
Action: New Ordnance steel, rolling block; smokeless powder action with case hardened frame
Magazine: None; single-shot
Barrel: 28"-30"; light weight, round steel barrel
Stock & Forearm: Plain varnished walnut, two-piece straight grip stock & forearm; steel buttplate; lipped forearm
Estimated Value: $270.00 - $340.00

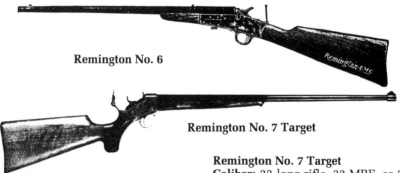

Remington No. 6

Remington No. 7 Target

Remington No. 6
Caliber: 22 short, long, or long rifle; 32 short & long RF
Action: Rolling-block; visible hammer; takedown model
Magazine: None; single-shot
Barrel: 20"; round tapered barrel
Stock & Forearm: Plain varnished walnut straight grip stock & forearm; steel buttplate
Estimated Value: $160.00 - $200.00

Remington No. 7 Target
Caliber: 22 long rifle, 32 MRF, or 25 Stevens RF
Action: Rolling block; visible hammer
Magazine: None; single-shot
Barrel: 24", 26", or 28"; half-octagon barrel
Stock & Forearm: Varnished checkered walnut pistol grip stock & forearm; capped pistol grip; rubber buttplate; lipped forearm
Estimated Value: $520.00 - $700.00

Remington-Lee Sporting

Remington-Lee Military

Remington-Lee Military Carbine

Remington-Lee Sporting
Caliber: 6mm U.S. Navy, 30-30 Sporting, 30-40 U.S. Government, 7mm Mauser, or 7.65mm Mauser
Action: Improved smokeless powder, bolt action; repeating
Magazine: 5-shot removable box
Barrel: 24" to 28"; smokeless powder, round steel barrel
Stock & Forearm: Checkered walnut one-piece semi-pistol grip stock & lipped forearm with finger groove on each side
Estimated Value: $360.00 - $450.00

Remington-Lee Military
Caliber: 30-40 Krag, 303 British, 6mm Lee Navy, 7mm Mauser, or 7.65 mm Mauser
Action: Improved smokeless powder, bolt action; repeating, rimless cartridges
Magazine: 5-shot removable box
Barrel: 29"; smokeless powder round steel barrel
Stock & Forearm: Plain walnut one-piece straight grip stock & long forearm; cleaning rod; barrel bands; wood hand guard
Estimated Value: $340.00 - $425.00

Remington-Lee Military Carbine
Similar to Remington-Lee Military except: 20" barrel; one barrel band
Estimated Value: $320.00 - $400.00

Remington Model 1907-15 RIFLE
Caliber: 8mm Lebel
Action: Smokeless powder bolt action; repeating; self-cocking striker with knurled top for uncocking & manual cocking
Magazine: 5-shot box
Barrel: 26" to 31" round with four groove rifling
Stock & Forearm: Plain varnished walnut one-piece stock & long forearm; barrel bands; cleaning rod in forearm. Left side of action marked "Remington MLE 1907-15"
Estimated Value: $240.00 - $300.00

Remington Model 1907-15 Carbine
Same as Remington Model 1907-15 Rifle except: 22" barrel; no barrel bands; short forearm
Estimated Value: $220.00 - $275.00

Remington

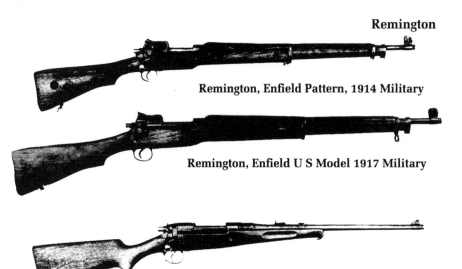

Remington, Enfield Pattern, 1914 Military

Remington, Enfield U S Model 1917 Military

Remington Model 30
(Intermediate Variety)

Remington Model 30 (Early Variety)
Caliber: 30-06 Government
Action: Improved 1917 Enfield bolt action; repeating; self-cocking when bolt is closed; hinged floor plate; side-safety
Magazine: 5-shot box
Barrel: 24"; light round
Stock & Forearm: Plain varnished walnut, one-piece pistol grip stock & lipped forearm with finger groves; steel buttplate; marked "Remington Arms Co. Inc., Remington Ilion Works, Ilion, N.Y. Made in U.S.A."
Estimated Value: $360.00 - $450.00

Remington Model 30
(Intermediate Variety)
Same as Model 30 (Early Variety) except: calibers 30-06 Government, 25, 30, 32, 35 Remington, or 7mm Mauser; 22" barrel length; also made in 20" barrel carbine; made from about 1926 to 1930
Estimated Value: $340.00 - $425.00

Remington, Enfield U.S. Model 1917 Military
Caliber: 30-06 Government, rimless
Action: Smokeless powder bolt action; repeating; self-cocking on down stroke of bolt handle; actions made with interchangeable parts
Magazine: 5-shot box
Barrel: 26"; round tapered
Stock & Forearm: Plain one-piece walnut modified pistol grip stock & full-length forearm with finger grooves; wood hand guard; two barrel bands; sling loops; bayonet lug; marked "Model of 1917," Remington & serial no. on bridge
Estimated Value: $290.00 - $360.00

Remington, Enfield Pattern, 1914 Military
Caliber: 303 British (rimmed)
Action: British smokeless powder bolt action; repeating; self-cocking on down stroke of bolt handle
Magazine: 5-shot box
Barrel: 26"; round tapered barrel
Stock & Forearm: Oil finished walnut, one-piece stock & forearm; wood hand guard; modified pistol grip stock; full-length forearm with two barrel bands
Estimated Value: $260.00 - $325.00

Remington

Remington Model 30 Express

Remington Model 34

Remington Model 30 Express
Caliber: 25, 30, 32, 35 Remington, 30-06 Government, or 7mm Mauser until 1936; after 1936 caliber 257 Roberts & 30-06 government only
Action: Bolt action; repeating; self-cocking; thumb safety
Magazine: 5-shot box
Barrel: 22" or 24"; round barrel
Stock & Forearm: Plain or checkered walnut pistol grip one-piece stock & lipped forearm; early models have grooved forearm
Estimated Value: $400.00 - $495.00

Remington Model 30R Carbine
Same as Model 30 Express except: 20" barrel; plain walnut one-piece stock and forearm
Estimated Value: $380.00 - $475.00

Remington Model 30S Sporting
Similar to Model 30 Express except: caliber 257 Roberts, 7mm Mauser, or 30-06; rear peep sight; special grade high-comb stock
Estimated Value: $400.00 - $500.00

Remington Model 33
Caliber: 22 short, long, or long rifle
Action: Bolt action; takedown model; exposed knurled cocking-piece
Magazine: None; single-shot
Barrel: 24"; round
Stock & Forearm: Plain varnished walnut one-piece pistol grip stock & forearm; made from about 1931 to 1936; finger grooves added to forearm in 1934
Estimated Value: $95.00 - $120.00

Remington Model 33 NRA Junior Target
Same as Model 33 except: post front sight; peep rear sight; equipped with 1" leather sling; swivels
Estimated Value: $120.00 - $150.00

Remington Model 34
Caliber: 22 short, long, or long rifle
Action: Bolt action; repeating; takedown model; self-cocking; thumb safety
Magazine: Tubular under barrel; 22 shorts, 17 longs, 15 long rifles
Barrel: 24"; round
Stock & Forearm: Plain wood, one-piece pistol grip stock & grooved forearm; made from about 1933 to 1935; also produced in Model 34 NRA target model with peep rear sight & sling swivels
Estimated Value: $125.00 - $155.00

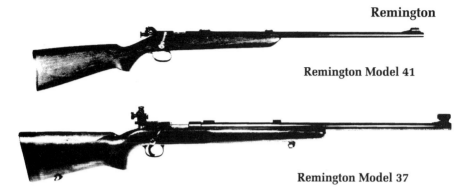

Remington Model 41

Remington Model 37

Remington Model 41
Caliber: 22 short, long, long rifle, or 22 WRF
Action: Bolt action; takedown model; exposed knurled cocking-piece
Magazine: None; single-shot
Barrel: 27"; round
Stock & Forearm: Plain one-piece pistol grip stock & forearm; hard rubber buttplate; made from about 1936 to 1940 in following models: 41 A - "Standard" model with open sights; 41 P - "Target" model with target sights; 41 AS - "Special" model chambered for 22 WRF; 41 SB - "Smoothbore" model; no rifling, chambered for 22 LR shot shell only
Estimated Value: $110.00 - $135.00

Remington Model 341 Sportsmaster
Caliber: 22 short, long, or long rifle
Action: Bolt action; repeating; takedown model; self-cocking; thumb safety
Magazine: Tubular under barrel; 22 shorts, 17 longs, 15 long rifles
Barrel: 27"; round
Stock & Forearm: Plain wood one-piece pistol grip stock & forearm
Estimated Value: $115.00 - $140.00

Remington Model 341 S Sportsmaster
Same as Model 341 Sportsmaster except: smooth bore for 22 shot cartridges
Estimated Value: $110.00 - $135.00

Remington Model 37 Rangemaster
Caliber: 22 long rifle
Action: Bolt action; repeating; self-cocking; thumb safety: adjustable trigger
Magazine: 5-shot clip & single-shot adapter
Barrel: 28"; heavy, semi-floating target barrel
Stock & Forearm: Lacquer finished heavy target, one-piece walnut stock & forearm; high flute comb stock with plain pistol grip & steel buttplate; early models had rounded beavertail forearm with one barrel band; barrel band dropped in 1938 & forearm modified
Estimated Value: $320.00 - $400.00

Remington Model 37 (1940 Model)
Similar to Model 37 Rangemaster except: improved trigger mechanism; re-designed stock; wide beavertail forearm; produced from about 1940 to 1955
Estimated Value: $350.00 - $435.00

Remington

Remington Model 510 Targetmaster

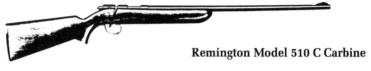

Remington Model 510 C Carbine

Remington Model 511

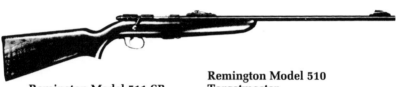

Remington Model 511 SB

Remington Model 511 Scoremaster
Caliber: 22 short, long, or long rifle
Action: Bolt action; repeating; self-cocking; thumb safety & cocking indicator; takedown model
Magazine: 6-shot clip; also 10-shot clip after 1952
Barrel: 25"; light, round
Stock & Forearm: Plain walnut one-piece pistol grip stock & forearm
Estimated Value: $95.00 - $120.00

Remington Model 511 SB
Same as Model 511 Scoremaster except: smooth bore for 22 shot cartridges
Estimated Value: $100.00 - $125.00

Remington Model 510 Targetmaster
Caliber: 22 short, long, or long rifle
Action: Bolt action; takedown model; selfcocking with thumb safety & cocking indicator
Magazine: None; single shot
Barrel: 25"; light, round
Stock & Forearm: Plain walnut one-piece pistol grip stock & forearm; made from about 1939 to 1962 in three models: 510 A Standard model; 510 P with peep sights; & 510 SB, a smooth-bore chambered for 22 shot shells
Estimated Value: $95.00 - $120.00

Remington Model 510 C Carbine
Same as Model 510 Targetmaster except: 21" barrel; made from about 1961 to 1962
Estimated Value: $80.00 - $100.00

Remington Model 512 Sportmaster

Remington Model 512 SB
Same as Model 512 Sportmaster except smooth bore for 22 shot cartridge
Estimated Value: $95.00 - $120.00

Remington Model 512 Sportmaster
Caliber: 22 short, long, or long rifle
Action: Bolt action; repeating; self cocking; thumb safety; cocking indicator
Magazine: Tubular under barrel; 22 shorts, 17 longs, 15 long rifles
Barrel: 25"; light, round
Stock & Forearm: Plain walnut one-piece pistol grip stock & forearm; composition buttplate
Estimated Value: $85.00 - $110.00

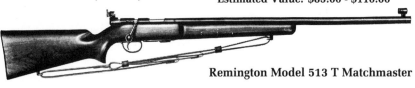

Remington Model 513 T Matchmaster

Remington Model 514

Remington Model 514
Caliber: 22 short, long, or long rifle
Action: Bolt action; takedown model; self-cocking
Magazine: None; single-shot
Barrel: 21" (514 BR), or 24"; light weight, round
Stock & Forearm: Plain walnut one-piece pistol grip stock & forearm; made in three models; 514 Standard Model; 514 P had target sights (peep rear sight); 514 BR Boys Rifle had 1" shorter stock & 21" barrel
Estimated Value: $70.00 - $90.00

Remington Model 513 T Matchmaster
Caliber: 22 long rifle
Action: Bolt action; repeating; self-cocking; side safety; cocking indicator; adjustable trigger
Magazine: 6-shot clip
Barrel: 27"; medium weight, round barrel; semi-floating type
Stock & Forearm: Plain, heavy, high fluted comb; lacquered walnut one-piece pistol grip stock & beavertail forearm
Estimated Value: $180.00 - $225.00

Remington Model 513 S Sporter Rifle
Similar to Model 513 T Matchmaster except: lighter checkered walnut one-piece sporting stock & forearm; ramp front sight & adjustable open rear sight
Estimated Value: $170.00 - $210.00

Remington

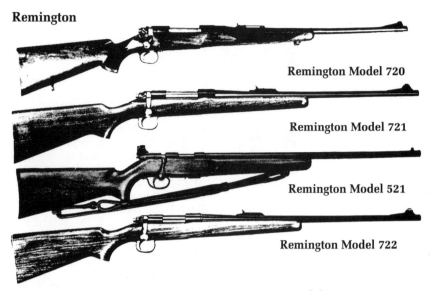

Remington Model 720

Remington Model 721

Remington Model 521

Remington Model 722

Remington Model 721
Caliber: 270, 30-06, or 300 mag.; after 1959, 280 Rem.
Action: Bolt action; repeating; self-cocking; side safety; adjustable trigger
Magazine: 4-shot box with fixed floor plate; 3-shot in 300 magnum
Barrel: 24" or 26"; round
Stock & Forearm: Checkered walnut or plain one-piece pistol grip stock & forearm; aluminum shotgun buttplate
Estimated Value: $200.00 - $250.00

Remington Model 521 TL Target
Caliber: 22 long rifle
Action: Bolt action; repeating; self-cocking; thumb safety; cocking indicator
Magazine: 5 or 10-shot clip
Barrel: 25"; medium weight, round barrel
Stock & Forearm: Heavy target one-piece pistol grip stock & beavertail forearm; varnished or oil finished; rubber buttplate; a low cost rifle intended for junior target shooter
Estimated Value: $100.00 - $125.00

Remington Model 720
Caliber: 257 Roberts, 270 Win., or 30-06 Government
Action: Bolt action; repeating; self-cocking; side safety
Magazine: 5-shot box; removable floor plate
Barrel: 20", 22", or 24"; round
Stock & Forearm: Checkered walnut one-piece pistol grip stock & forearm
Estimated Value: $255.00 - $320.00

Remington Model 722
Caliber: 257 Roberts or 300 Savage; 222 Rem. (after 1949); 308 Win. & 244 Rem. (after 1955); 222 Rem. mag. (after 1957); 243 Win. (after 1959)
Action: Bolt action; repeating; self-cocking; side-safety; fixed floor plate; adjustable trigger
Magazine: 4-shot box; 5-shot in 222 magnum
Barrel: 22" or 24"; round
Stock & Forearm: Checkered or plain varnished walnut one-piece pistol grip stock & forearm; after 1950 option of high-comb stock & tapered forearm
Estimated Value: $220.00 - $275.00

Remington

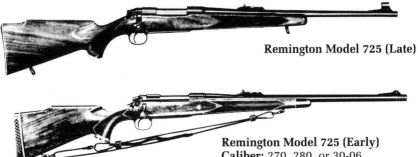

Remington Model 725 (Late)

Remington Model 725 Magnum

Remington Model 725 Magnum
Caliber: 375 or 458 Win. magnum
Action: Bolt action; repeating; self-cocking; thumb safety
Magazine: 3-shot box
Barrel: 26"; heavy, round barrel with muzzle brake
Stock & Forearm: Fancy reinforced, checkered walnut Monte Carlo one-piece pistol grip stock & forearm; stock with cap & rubber recoil pad; black tipped forearm
Estimated Value: $480.00 - $600.00

Remington Model 725 (Early)
Caliber: 270, 280, or 30-06
Action: Bolt action; repeating; self-cocking; thumb safety
Magazine: 4-shot box
Barrel: 22"; round
Stock & Forearm: Checkered walnut Monte Carlo one-piece pistol grip stock & forearm; capped grip stock with shotgun buttplate & sling loops
Estimated Value: $280.00 - $350.00

Remington Model 725 (Late)
Same as Model 725 (Early) except: also in calibers 243 Win., 244 Rem., or 222 Rem.; 24" barrel in 222 Rem. and aluminum buttplate on all calibers; made from about 1960 to 1961
Estimated Value: $300.00 - $380.00

Remington Model 10 Nylon

Remington Model 10 SB
Same as Model 10 Nylon except: smooth bore; chambered for 22 shot shells
Estimated Value: $65.00 - $80.00

Remington Model 10 Nylon
Caliber: 22 short, long, or long rifle
Action: Bolt action; self-cocking striker with indicator; slide safety
Magazine: None; single-shot
Barrel: 19½"; round
Stock & Forearm: Nylon checkered one-piece pistol grip stock & forearm; shotgun buttplate
Estimated Value: $60.00 - $75.00

Pocket Guide to Rifles

Remington

Remington Nylon 11

Remington Nylon 12

Remington Nylon 11
Caliber: 22 short, long, or long rifle
Action: Bolt action; repeating; self-cocking; cocking indicator
Magazine: 6 or 10-shot clip
Barrel: 19½"; round
Stock & Forearm: Polished brown checkered nylon pistol grip one-piece stock & forearm; white liners & two white diamond inlays on each side; hand guard
Estimated Value: $70.00 - $90.00

Remington Nylon 12
Similar to Remington Nylon 11 except: tubular magazine under barrel holds 14 to 21 shots
Estimated Value: $75.00 - $95.00

Remington Model 600

Remington Model 660

Remington Model 600 Magnum
Similar to the Model 600 except: magnum calibers; 4-shot magazine; walnut & beechwood stock; swivels; recoil pad
Estimated Value: $260.00 - $325.00

Remington Model 660
Similar to the Model 600 except: 20" barrel without rib
Estimated Value: $225.00 - $280.00

Remington Model 600
Caliber: 6mm Rem., 222 Rem., 243 Win., 308 Win., or 35 Rem.
Action: Bolt action; repeating
Magazine: 5-shot box
Barrel: 18½"; ventilated rib
Stock & Forearm: Checkered walnut Monte Carlo one-piece pistol grip stock & forearm
Estimated Value: $220.00 - $275.00

Remington Model 660 Magnum
Similar to the Model 600 Magnum except: 20" barrel without rib; beaded front sight
Estimated Value: $280.00 - $350.00

Remington Model 580

Remington Model 581

Remington Model 582

Remington Model 788

Remington Model 580 SB
Same as Model 580 except: smooth
bore for 22 long rifle shot shell
Estimated Value: $70.00 - $85.00

Remington Model 580
Caliber: 22 short, long, or long rifle
Action: Bolt action; self-cocking
striker
Magazine: None; single-shot
Barrel: 24"; round
Stock & Forearm: Plain wood Monte
Carlo one-piece pistol grip stock &
forearm; plastic shotgun buttplate
Estimated Value: $65.00 - $80.00

Remington Model 581 & 581 S
Caliber: 22 short, long, or long rifle
Action: Bolt action; repeating; self-
cocking; thumb safety
Magazine: 5-shot clip; single shot
adapter
Barrel: 24"; round
Stock & Forearm: Plain wood Monte
Carlo one-piece pistol grip stock &
forearm; made from about 1967 to
1983; reintroduced in 1986 as
"Sportsman" 581-S
Estimated Value: $115.00 - $150.00

Remington Model 582
Same as Model 581 except: 14 to 20-
shot tubular magazine under barrel
Estimated Value: $125.00 - $160.00

Remington Model 788
Caliber: 222, 22-250, 223 Rem., 6mm
Rem., 243 Win., 308 Win., or 7mm-
08 Rem. (added 1980)
Action: Bolt action; repeating; self-
cocking; thumb safety
Magazine: 5-shot clip in 222; 4-shot
clip in other calibers
Barrel: 24"; round tapered barrel in
calibers 222, 22-250 & 223 Rem.; 22"
barrel in other calibers; 18½" barrel
available 1980
Stock & Forearm: Monte Carlo one-
piece pistol grip stock & forearm;
current model has fluted comb &
wider pistol grip & forearm
Estimated Value: $200.00 - $250.00

Remington

Remington Model 591

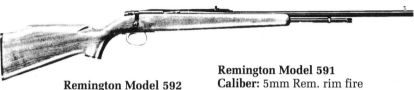

Remington Model 592

Remington Model 592
Same as Model 591 except; 10-shot tubular magazine under barrel
Estimated Value: $155.00 - $190.00

Remington Model 591
Caliber: 5mm Rem. rim fire
Action: Bolt action; repeating; self-cocking; thumb safety
Magazine: 4-shot clip
Barrel: 24"; round
Stock & Forearm: One-piece plain hardwood Monte Carlo stock & forearm
Estimated Value: $145.00 - $180.00

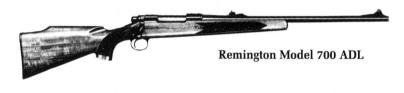

Remington Model 700 ADL

Remington Model 700 BDL Custom

Remington Model 700 BDL
Similar to Model 700 ADL except: custom deluxe grade with black forearm tip; sling strap; additional calibers: 17 Rem., 223 Rem., 264 Win. magnum, 300 Win. magnum, or 338 Win. magnum; add $25.00 for magnum calibers, $50.00 for left hand model
Estimated Value: $310.00 - $390.00

Remington Model 700 ADL
& 700 ADL-LS
Caliber: 222, 22-250, 6mm Rem., 243 Win., 25-06 Rem. 270 Win., 7mm Rem. mag., 308 Win., or 30-06
Action: Bolt action; repeating; self-cocking; thumb safety; checkered bolt handle
Magazine: 4 to 6-shot box magazine
Barrel: 22" or 24"; round tapered barrel
Stock & Forearm: Checkered walnut Monte Carlo pistol grip, one-piece stock & forearm; 700 ADL-LS has laminated stock; add $50.00 for laminated stock; add $25.00 for magnum or swivels & sling
Estimated Value: $265.00 - $330.00

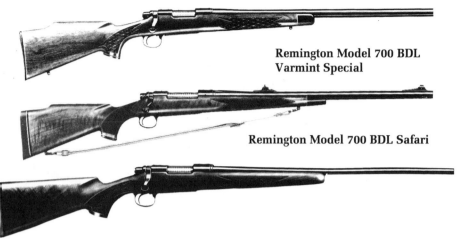

Remington Model 700 BDL Varmint Special

Remington Model 700 BDL Safari

Remington Model 700 BDL Classic

Remington Model 700 BDL Classic
Similar to 700 BDL except: stock styling changes; calibers 22-250 Rem., 6mm Rem., 243 Win., 270 Win., or 30-06; add $20.00 for magnum; a limited number available in 1981 in 7mm magnum; 1982, 257 Roberts; 1983, 300 H & H magnum; 1984, 250 Savage; 1985, 350 Rem. magnum; 1986, 264 Win. magnum; 1992, 220 Swift
Estimated Value: $310.00 - $390.00

Remington Model 700 BDL Varmint Special
Similar to 700 BDL except: heavy barrel in 22 Rem., 22-250 Rem., 223 Rem., 6mm Rem., 243 Win., 25-06 Rem., 7mm-08, or 308 Win.
Estimated Value: $330.00 - $415.00

Remington Model 700 BDL Safari
Similar to Model 700 BDL except: 375 H & H magnum or 458 Win. magnum; recoil pad; 8mm Rem. magnum caliber added in 1986
Estimated Value: $420.00 - $525.00

Remington Model 700 "Mountain Rifle"

Remington Model 700 "Mountain Rifle"
Similar to 700 BDL except: 270 Win., 280 Rem. or 30-06 caliber; 25-06 Rem. added in 1992
Estimated Value: $310.00 - $390.00

Remington Model 700FS
Similar to Model 700ADL except: it has a Kelvar® reinforced fiberglass stock (gray or gray camo); in calibers: 243 Win., 270 Win., 30-06, or 308 Win.; 7mm Rem. magnum introduced in 1987
Estimated Value: $375.00 - $465.00

Remington

Remington Model 700AS

Remington Model 700
Varmint Synthetic

Remington Model 700RS
Similar to the Model 700BDL except: with a DuPont Rynite® stock; textured finish; calibers: 270 Win. or 280 Rem.; 30-06; introduced in 1987
Estimated Value: $325.00 - $410.00

Remington Model 700 Varmint Synthetic
Caliber: 22-250 Rem., 223 Rem., or 308 Win.
Action: Bolt action; repeating; thumb safety
Magazine: 4-shot box
Barrel: 24"; black matte finish
Stock & Forearm: Composite Kevlar, fiberglass, and graphite; textured black and gray non-reflective finish; swivels
Estimated Value: $650.00 - $825.00

Remington Model 700AS
Caliber: 22-250, 243 Win., 270 Win., 280 Rem., 30-06 Win., 7mm Rem. magnum, or 300 Weatherby magnum; add 4% for mag. calibers
Action: Bolt action; repeating; thumb safety
Magazine: 4-shot box in all calibers except 7mm Rem. magnum & 300 Weatherby magnum, which are 3-shot
Barrel: 22"; blued in all calibers except: 22-250, 7mm Rem. magnum & 300 Weatherby magnum which have 24" blued barrel
Stock & Forearm: Synthetic resin, one-piece pistol grip stock & forearm; solid recoil pad
Estimated Value: $320.00 - $400.00

**Remington Model 700
Stainless Synthetic**

**Remington Model 700
Camo Synthetic**
Caliber: 22-250 Rem., 243 Win., 270 Win., 280 Rem., 7mm-08 Rem., 7mm Rem. magnum, 30-06, 308 Win., or 300 Wby. magnum
Action: Bolt action; repeating; thumb safety
Magazine: 4-shot box
Barrel: 22" or 24"; camouflaged
Stock & Forearm: Camouflaged synthetic one-piece pistol grip stock and forearm; recoil pad; swivels
Estimated Value: $335.00 - $425.00

Remington Model 700 Stainless Synthetic
Caliber: 25-06 Rem., 270 Win., 280 Rem., 30-06 Sprg., 7mm Rem. magnum, 7mm Wby. magnum, 300 Win. magnum, or 338 Win. mag.
Action: Bolt action; repeating; thumb safety
Magazine: 4-shot box
Barrel: 24"; stainless steel, matte finish
Stock & Forearm: Black textured, non-reflective synthetic stock with checkering on pistol grip and forearm; swivels
Estimated Value: $320.00 - $400.00

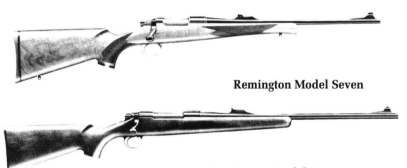

Remington Model Seven

Remington Sportsman 78

Remington Sportsman 78
Similar to the Model 700 except: lesser quality finish; hardwood with no checkering; 22" barrel; 270 Win. & 30-06 calibers; introduced in 1984; 243 & 308 calibers added in 1985; 223 caliber added in 1986
Estimated Value: $220.00 - $275.00

Remington Model Seven
Caliber: 222 Rem., 223 Rem., 243 Win., 6mm Rem., 7mm-08 Rem., or 308 Win.
Action: Bolt action; repeating
Magazine: 4 or 5-shot box with steel floor plate
Barrel: 18½"; tapered
Stock & Forearm: Checkered walnut one-piece pistol grip stock & slightly lipped forearm; recoil pad; swivels
Estimated Value: $310.00 - $390.00

Remington

Remington Model 40X Target

Remington Model 40XR

Remington Model 40XB

Remington Model 40XBBR

Remington Model 40X Target
Caliber: 22 long rifle, 222 Rem., 308, or 30-06; others on special order
Action: Bolt action; single-shot; self-cocking; thumb safety; adjustable trigger
Magazine: None; single-shot
Barrel: 28"; standard or heavy round barrel with bedding device in forearm
Stock & Forearm: Oiled, plain, heavy target one-piece pistol grip stock; rubber shotgun buttplate; high fluted comb stock
Estimated Value: $360.00 - $450.00

Remington Model 40XR
A target rifle similar to the Model 40X Target except: widened stock & forearm; adjustable buttplate; hand stop; introduced in the late 1970's. 22 long rifle only; add $120.00 for Kelvar® stock
Estimated Value: $560.00 - $700.00

Remington Model 40XB Rangemaster
Similar to the Model 40X Target except: stainless steel barrel; calibers 222 Rem., 22-250 Rem., 243 Win., 6mm Rem., 25-06 Rem., 7mm Rem. magnum, 7.62mm NATO, 30-06, 30-338, or 300 Win. magnum; add $50.00 for repeating model
Estimated Value: $600.00 - $730.00

Remington Model 40XB KS
Similar to the Model 40XB Rangemaster except: DuPont Kevlar reinforced stock, free-floating barrel and match-grade trigger; left or right hand models; single shot or repeating models
Estimated Value: $660.00 - $800.00

Remington Model 40XBBR
Similar to the Model 40XB Rangemaster except: 20" or 24" barrel
Estimated Value: $660.00 - $750.00

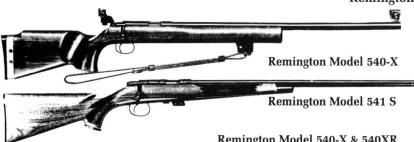

Remington Model 540-X

Remington Model 541 S

Remington Model 541 S Custom & 541-T
Caliber: 22 short, long, or long rifle
Action: Bolt action; repeating; self-cocking; thumb safety
Magazine: 5-shot clip
Barrel: 24"
Stock & Forearm: One-piece checkered pistol grip stock & forearm; made from about 1972 to 1983; reintroduced in 1986 as Model 541-T
Estimated Value: $215.00 - $265.00

Remington Model 540-X & 540XR
Caliber: 22 long rifle
Action: Bolt action; single shot; self-cocking striker; slide safety; adjustable match trigger
Magazine: None; single-shot
Barrel: 26"; heavy target barrel
Stock & Forearm: Full pistol grip, heavy wood one-piece stock & forearm; thumb-grooved stock with 4-way adjustable buttplate rail; a heavy rifle designed for bench shooting
Estimated Value: $190.00 - $255.00

Remington Nylon 76

Remington Model No. 12 Rifle
Caliber: 22 short, long, or long rifle
Action: Slide action; hammerless; takedown model
Magazine: 10 to 15-shot tubular, under barrel
Barrel: 22" or 24"; round or octagon
Stock & Forearm: Plain or engraved; varnished plain or checkered, straight or pistol grip, walnut stock with rubber or steel buttplate; forearm grooved or checkered walnut; made from about 1909 to 1936 in four grades; higher grades had checkering & engraving; prices are for (plain) standard grade
Estimated Value: $180.00 - $225.00

Remington Nylon 76
Caliber: 22 long rifle
Action: Lever-action; repeating; side ejection; lever under stock operates sliding bolt which ejects empty case, chambers cartridge from magazine & cocks concealed striker; safety located on top of stock behind receiver
Magazine: 14-shot tubular magazine in stock
Barrel: 19½"; round
Stock & Forearm: Checkered nylon two-piece pistol grip stock & lipped forearm; nylon hand guard over barrel; the only lever action repeater made by Remington Arms Co
Estimated Value: $115.00 - $150.00

Remington

Remington Model 14

Remington Model 14 R

Remington Model 14 Rifle
Caliber: 25, 30, 32, or 35 Rem.
Action: Slide action; hammerless; takedown model
Magazine: 5-shot tubular, under barrel
Barrel: 22"; round
Stock & Forearm: Plain or checkered walnut pistol grip stock & grooved or checkered forearm; made in four grades; higher grades had checkering & engraving; prices are for (plain) standard grade
Estimated Value: $255.00 - $320.00

Remington Model 14½ Rifle
Similar to Model 14 rifle except: calibers 38-40 or 44-40; 22½" barrel; 11-shot magazine; discontinued about 1925; standard grade only
Estimated Value: $320.00 - $400.00

Remington Model 14½ Carbine
Same as Model 14½ rifle except: 18½" barrel; 9-shot magazine
Estimated Value: $340.00 - $425.00

Remington Model 14 R Carbine
Same as Model 14 rifle except: 18½" barrel; straight grip stock; standard grade only
Estimated Value: $240.00 - $300.00

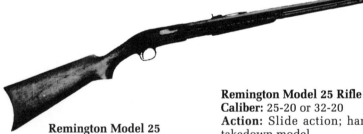

Remington Model 25

Remington Model 25 R Carbine
Same as Model 25 Rifle except: 18½" barrel; straight grip stock; 6-shot magazine; standard grade only
Estimated Value: $280.00 - $350.00

Remington Model 25 Rifle
Caliber: 25-20 or 32-20
Action: Slide action; hammerless; takedown model
Magazine: 10-shot tubular
Barrel: 24"
Stock & Forearm: Checkered or plain walnut pistol grip stock and grooved or checkered slide handle; made from about 1923 to 1936 in four grades; higher grades had checkering & engraving; prices are for (plain) standard grades
Estimated Value: $290.00 - $360.00

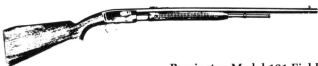

Remington Model 121 Fieldmaster

Remington Model 141 Gamemaster
Caliber: 30, 32, or 35 Rem.
Action: Slide action; hammerless; takedown model
Magazine: 5-shot tubular, under barrel
Barrel: 24"; round
Stock & Forearm: Checkered or plain walnut pistol grip stock & grooved or checkered semi-beavertail slide handle; made in four grades; higher grades have checkered pistol grip stock & forearm & engraving; priced for (plain) standard grade
Estimated Value: $265.00 - $330.00

Remington 141 R Carbine
Same as Model 141 Gamemaster except: 18½" barrel; standard grade
Estimated Value: $260.00 - $325.00

Remington Model 121 Fieldmaster
Caliber: 22 short, long, or long rifle
Action: Slide action; hammerless; takedown model
Magazine: Tubular, under barrel; 20 shorts, 15 longs, or 14 long rifle
Barrel: 24"; round
Stock & Forearm: Checkered or plain walnut pistol grip stock & grooved or checkered semi-beavertail slide handle; made in four grades; higher grades are checkered & engraved; priced for (plain) standard grade
Estimated Value: $210.00 - $260.00

Remington Model 121 SB
Same as Model 121 except smooth bore barrel for 22 shot cartridges
Estimated Value: $220.00 - $275.00

Remington Model 121 S
Similar to Model 121 except: caliber 22 Rem. special only; 12-shot magazine; standard grade
Estimated Value: $215.00 - $265.00

Remington Model 572 BDL

Remington 572 BDL Fieldmaster
Deluxe version of the 572A Fieldmaster
Estimated Value: $135.00 - $165.00

Remington Model 572 SB
Same as Model 572A Fieldmaster except: smooth bore for 22 shot cartridges
Estimated Value: $120.00 - $150.00

Remington Model 572 A Fieldmaster
Caliber: 22 short, long, or long rifle
Action: Slide action; hammerless; solid frame; side ejection
Magazine: 14 to 20-shot tubular, under barrel
Barrel: 21" & 24"; round tapered
Stock & Forearm: Checkered or plain walnut pistol grip stock & grooved or checkered slide handle
Estimated Value: $120.00 - $160.00

Remington

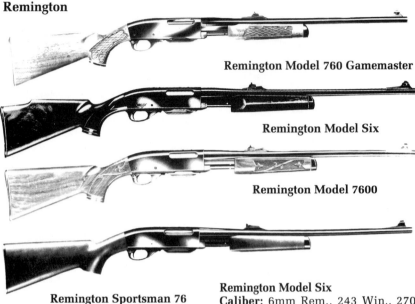

Remington Model 760 Gamemaster

Remington Model Six

Remington Model 7600

Remington Sportsman 76

Remington Model 760 Gamemaster & 760 Carbine
Caliber: 30-06, 308, 300 Savage, 35 Rem., 280, 270 Win., 257 Roberts, 244 Rem., 243 Win., 6mm Rem., 223, or 222
Action: Slide action; hammerless; side ejection; solid frame; cross-bolt safety
Magazine: 4-shot box
Barrel: 22"; round tapered; 18½" on carbine
Stock & Forearm: Checkered or plain walnut pistol grip stock & grooved checkered semi-beavertail slide handle
Estimated Value: $225.00 - $300.00

Remington Model 760 BDL Gamemaster
Similar to Model 760 Gamemaster except: basketweave checkering, Monte Carlo stock; 30-06, 308, or 270 caliber
Estimated Value: $230.00 - $310.00

Remington Model Six
Caliber: 6mm Rem., 243 Win., 270 Win., 30-06, or 308 Win.
Action: Slide action; hammerless; repeating
Magazine: 4-shot clip
Barrel: 22"; blued
Stock & Forearm: Checkered walnut Monte Carlo pistol grip stock & slide handle; black grip cap & fore-end tip; recessed finger groove in slide handle; high-gloss finish; custom grades were available at increased prices
Estimated Value: $300.00 - $400.00

Remington Model 7600
Similar to the Model Six except: no Monte Carlo stock or cheekpiece; design checkering
Estimated Value: $290.00 - $360.00

Remington Sportsman 76
Similar to the Model 7600 except: lesser quality finish; hardwood with no checkering; 22" barrel; 30-06 caliber only
Estimated Value: $240.00 - $300.00

Remington Model No. 16

Remington Model No. 16
Caliber: 22 Rem. automatic
Action: Semi-auto; hammerless; solid breech; sliding bolt; side ejection; takedown model
Magazine: 15-shot tubular, in stock
Barrel: 22"; round
Stock & Forearm: Plain or engraved; varnished, plain or checkered, straight grip, two-piece walnut stock & forearm; steel buttplate; blunt lip on forearm; made in four grades: A, C, D & F; priced for standard grade
Estimated Value: $240.00 - $300.00

Remington Model No. 8
Caliber: 25, 30, 32, or 35 Rem.
Action: Semi-automatic; top ejection; takedown model; solid breech; sliding barrel type; for smokeless powder
Magazine: 5-shot detachable box
Barrel: 22"; round
Stock & Forearm: Plain or engraved; varnished, plain or checkered, two-piece walnut straight grip stock & forearm; rubber or steel buttplate & lipped forearm; made in five grades: A, C, D, E & F; priced for standard grade
Estimated Value: $285.00 - $360.00

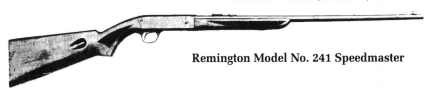

Remington Model No. 241 Speedmaster

Remington Model 24
Caliber: 22 long rifle only or 22 short only
Action: Semi-auto; hammerless; solid breech; sliding bolt; bottom ejection
Magazine: tubular in stock; 15-shot in 22 short; 10-shot in 22 long rifle
Barrel: 19"; round
Stock & Forearm: Plain or engraved; varnished, plain or checkered, two-piece walnut semi-pistol grip stock & forearm; steel buttplate with lipped forearm; made in five grades: A, C, D, E & F; priced for standard grade
Estimated Value: $185.00 - $230.00

Remington Model 241 Speedmaster
Caliber: 22 long rifle only or 22 short only
Action: Semi-auto; hammerless; solid breech; bottom ejection; takedown type; sliding bolt action; thumb safety
Magazine: tubular in stock; 15-shot in 22 short; 10-shot in 22 long rifle
Barrel: 24"; round
Stock & Forearm: Plain or engraved; varnished walnut, plain or checkered, two-piece pistol grip stock & semi-beavertail forearm; made in five grades: A, B, D, E & F; priced for standard grade
Estimated Value: $210.00 - $260.00

Remington

Remington Model 550-2G Gallery

Remington Model 550 A
Caliber: 22 short, long, or long rifle
Action: Semi-automatic; hammer-less; side ejection; solid breech; sliding bolt; floating power piston which permits using 22 short, long, or long rifle interchangeable & still function as semi-automatic; takedown-type with thumb safety
Magazine: tubular, under barrel; 20-shot in 22 short; 16-shot in 22 long; 15-shot in 22 long rifle
Barrel: 24"; round
Stock & Forearm: One-piece plain varnished pistol grip stock & forearm; hard rubber buttplate; replaced the Model 241, because it was less expensive to produce
Estimated Value: $100.00 - $135.00

Remington Model 550-2G Gallery
Similar to Model 550 A except: chambered for 22 short caliber only
Estimated Value: $115.00 - $145.00

Remington Model 81 Woodsmaster
Caliber: , 25, 30, 32, 35 Rem., 30, 32, 35, or 300 Savage
Action: Semi-automatic; top ejection; takedown model; solid breech; sliding barrel type
Magazine: 5-shot detachable box
Barrel: 22"; round
Stock & Forearm: Plain or engraved; varnished walnut, plain or checkered two-piece pistol grip stock & forearm; rubber buttplate & semi-beavertail style forearm; made in five grades: A, B, D, E & F; priced for standard grade
Estimated Value: $265.00 - $330.00

Remington Model 740 A Woodsmaster

Remington Model 740 A Woodsmaster
Caliber: 30-06 or 308
Action: Semi-automatic; gas operated; side ejection; hammerless
Magazine: 4-shot detachable box
Barrel: 22"; round
Stock & Forearm: Plain pistol grip stock & forearm; semi-beavertail forearm with finger grooves
Estimated Value: $220.00 - $275.00

Remington Model 740 ADL Deluxe Grade
Same as Model 740 A except: deluxe checkered stock & forearm; also grip cap & sling swivels
Estimated Value: $230.00 - $290.00

Remington Model 740 BDL Special Grade
Similar to Model 740 ADL Deluxe Grade except: stock & forearm have deluxe finish on select wood
Estimated Value: $225.00 - $300.00

Remington Model 552 BDL Deluxe Speedmaster

Remington Model 552 BDL Deluxe Speedmaster
Same as Model 552A Speedmaster except: high-quality finished, checkered stock & forearm; ramp front sight & adjustable rear for elevation & windage
Estimated Value: $125.00 - $160.00

Remington Model 552 GS Gallery Special
Same as Model 552A Speedmaster except: 22 caliber short only
Estimated Value: $120.00 - $150.00

Remington Model 552 A Speedmaster
Caliber: 22 short, long, or long rifle, interchangeably
Action: Semi-automatic; hammerless; side ejection; solid breech; sliding bolt; floating power piston which permits using 22 short, long, long rifle cartridges interchangeably
Magazine: tubular, under barrel; 20-shot in 22 short, 16-shot in 22 long, or 15-shot in long rifle
Barrel: 21" & 23"; round, tapered
Stock & Forearm: Plain one-piece pistol grip stock & semi-beavertail forearm; hard composition checkered buttplate
Estimated Value: $115.00 - $150.00

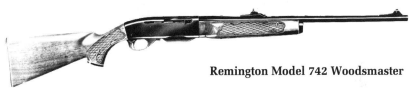

Remington Model 742 Woodsmaster

Remington Model 742 Woodsmaster
Caliber: 243 Win., 6mm Rem., 280 Rem., 308, or 30-06
Action: Semi-automatic; hammerless; side ejection; gas operated sliding bolt
Magazine: 4-shot detachable box
Barrel: 22"; round, tapered
Stock & Forearm: Plain or checkered & standard or deluxe finish two-piece walnut stock & semi-beavertail forearm; aluminum buttplate. In 1969 Remington advertised many fancy grades; priced for standard grade
Estimated Value: $260.00 - $325.00

Remington Model 742 Woodsmaster Carbine
Same as Model 742 Woodsmaster except: 18½" barrel; calibers 280, 30-06, or 308
Estimated Value: $255.00 - $320.00

Remington Model 742 BDL Woodsmaster
Same as Model 742 Woodsmaster except: calibers 30-06 or 308 only; left or right hand models; checkered Monte Carlo stock; black tipped forearm
Estimated Value: $270.00 - $340.00

Remington

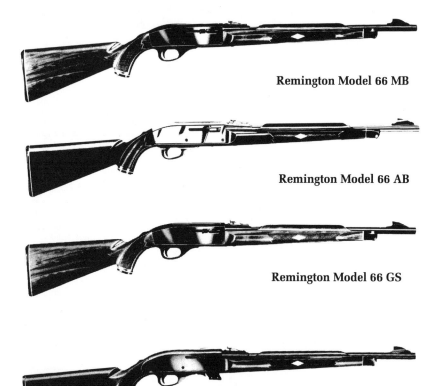

Remington Model 66 MB

Remington Model 66 AB

Remington Model 66 GS

Remington Model 10 C

Remington Model 66 AB & 66 BD
Same as Remington Model 66 MB except: black stock & forearm with chrome plated barrel & receiver covers; Model BD has black receiver
Estimated Value: $85.00 - $110.00

Remington Model 66 MB & 66 SG
Caliber: 22 long rifle
Action: Semi-automatic; side ejection; solid breech; sliding bolt
Magazine: 14-shot tubular, in stock
Barrel: 20"; round
Stock & Forearm: Du-Pont Zytel® nylon, brown one-piece receiver, stock & forearm; checkered pistol grip stock & lipped forearm which covers top of barrel; model 66 SG - Seneca Green
Estimated Value: $85.00 - $110.00

Remington Model 66 GS
Similar to the Model 66 MB except: chambered for 22 short only (Gallery Special)
Estimated Value: $80.00 - $100.00

Remington Model 10 C
Same as Remington Model 66 MB except: 10-shot removable box magazine
Estimated Value: $75.00 - $100.00

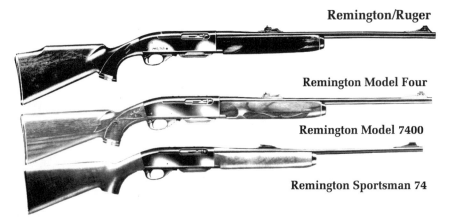

Remington Model Four

Remington Model 7400

Remington Sportsman 74

Remington Model 7400
Similar to the Model Four except: no Monte Carlo stock; design checkering
Estimated Value: $300.00 - $375.00

Remington Sportsman 74
Similar to the Model 7400 except: lesser quality finish; hardwood with no checkering; 22" barrel; 30-06 caliber only
Estimated Value: $240.00 - $320.00

Remington Model Four
Caliber: 6mm Rem., 243 Win., 270 Win., 280 Rem. (7mm Express Rem), 30-06, or 308 Win.
Action: Semi-automatic; side ejection; gas operated
Magazine: 4-shot clip
Barrel: 22"; blued
Stock & Forearm: Checkered walnut Monte Carlo pistol grip stock & forearm; black grip cap & fore-end tip; recessed finger groove in forearm; highgloss finish
Estimated Value: $320.00 - $430.00

Ruger

Ruger No. 1 Standard 1 B

Ruger No. 1 Light Sporter

Ruger No. 1 Light Sporter 1A
Similar to No. 1 in 243, 270, 30-06 or 7x57mm only; 22" barrel
Estimated Value: $380.00 - $475.00

Ruger No. 1 Standard 1 B
Caliber: 22-250, 220 Swift, 223, 243, 25-06, 6mm Rem., 257 Roberts, 280, 270, 30-06, 7mm Rem. mag., 300 Win. Mag., or 338 Win. mag.
Action: Falling block; under lever; single shot; hammerless
Magazine: None; single-shot
Barrel: 26"; tapered
Stock & Forearm: Checkered walnut pistol grip stock & forearm; swivels
Estimated Value: $380.00 - $475.00

Ruger

Ruger No. 1 Medium Sporter

Ruger No. 1 Tropical

Ruger Model No. 1 International

Ruger No. 1 Special Varminter 1 V

Ruger No. 3

Ruger No. 1 Medium Sporter 1 S
Similar to No. 1 Light Sporter
except: heavier calibers, 7mm, 338,
300, or 45-70; 22" or 26" barrel
Estimated Value: $380.00 - $475.00

Ruger No. 1 Special Varminter 1 V
Similar to No. 1 except: 22-250, 220
Swift, 223, 25-06, or 6mm; heavy 24"
barrel
Estimated Value: $380.00 - $475.00

Ruger No. 1 Tropical 1 H
A 24" barrel version of No. 1 in 375
H&H magnum or 458 magnum only
Estimated Value: $380.00 - $475.00

Ruger Model No. 1
International RSI
Similar to the No. 1 except: 20"
barrel with full-length forearm;
calibers 243 Win., 30-06, 270 Win.,
or 7x57mm
Estimated Value: $395.00 - $490.00

Ruger No. 3
Caliber: 22 Hornet, 30-40 Krag, 45-
70, 223, 375 Win., or 44 mag.
Action: Falling block, under lever;
hammerless; single shot
Magazine: None; single-shot
Barrel: 22"; blued
Stock & Forearm: Plain walnut
straight grip stock & forearm; barrel
band
Estimated Value: $280.00 - $350.00

Ruger Model 77

Ruger 77 Round Top

Ruger 77 International

Ruger 77 Varmint

Ruger Model 77R, 77RS, 77RS Tropical
Caliber: 220 Swift, 22-250, 25-06, 243 Win., 257, 270 Win., 280 Rem., 7mm Rem. mag., 7x57mm, 300 mag., 30-06, 35 Whelen, 338 mag., or 458 Win. mag. (Tropical)
Action: Bolt action; repeating; either short or magnum action
Magazine: 5-shot box with hinged floor plate; 4-shot in magnum calibers
Barrel: 22" or 24"; blued
Stock & Forearm: Checkered walnut, pistol grip, one-piece stock & tapered forearm; recoil pad; add 16% for 458 magnum (Tropical)
Estimated Value: $335.00 - $420.00

Ruger 77V Varmint, M-77 Varmint
Similar to Model 77 in 22-250, 220 Swift, 243, 6mm, 308, or 25-06 calibers; 24" heavy barrel or 26" tapered barrel
Estimated Value: $340.00 - $430.00

Ruger 77 Round Top, M-77ST
Similar to Model 77 except: round top receiver & open sights
Estimated Value: $280.00 - $350.00

Ruger Model 77 International, M-77RSI
Similar to the Model 77 except: 18½" barrel; full-length Mannlicher-type forearm; 22-250, 250-3000, 243, 308, 270, or 30-06 caliber
Estimated Value: $370.00 - $465.00

Ruger

Ruger Model 77RL Ultra Light

Ruger Model 77RL Ultra Light
Similar to the Model 77R except: 20" barrel; Caliber 22-250, 243, 270, 250-3000, 257, 30-06, or 308
Estimated Value: $340.00 - $425.00

Ruger Model 77/22
Caliber: 22 long rifle or 22 magnum
Action: Bolt action; repeating; three position safety
Magazine: Detachable rotary magazine; 10-shot (22 long rifle); 9-shot (22 magnum)
Barrel: 20"; blued or stainless steel
Stock & Forearm: Checkered walnut, one piece, pistol grip stock and forearm; stainless steel models have all-weather stock (DuPont Zytel®); deduct 18% for all-weather stock with blued barrel; add 4.5% for all-weather stock and stainless steel barrel
Estimated Value: $240.00 - $300.00

Ruger Model 77 Mark IIR

Ruger Model 77 Mark IIRL, IIVRL
Similar to the Model 77 Mark IIR except: calibers 223, 243, or 308; 20" barrel; black fore-end tip
Estimated Value: $355.00 - $445.00

Ruger Model 77 Mark IIRS, IIVRS
Same as the Model 77 Mark IIR except: calibers 6mm, 243, or 308
Estimated Value: $370.00 - $460.00

Ruger Model 77 Mark IIRP, IIVRP
Same as the Model 77 Mark IIR except: all stainless steel with all-weather fiberglass stock (DuPont Zytel®) with grooved inserts on the pistol grip & fore-end sides; calibers 223, 243, or 308
Estimated Value: $335.00 - $420.00

Ruger Model 77 Mark IIR & IIVR
Caliber: 223, 6mm, 243, 270, 30-06, 7mm, or 308
Action: Bolt action; repeating; stainless steel bolt with three position swing back safety (in rear position bolt is locked & gun will not fire; in center position the bolt will operate but gun will not fire; in forward position bolt will operate & gun will fire); short action bolt
Magazine: 4-shot box with hinged floor plate
Barrel: 22"; blued
Stock & Forearm: Checkered walnut, one-piece pistol grip stock & tapered forearm
Estimated Value: $335.00 - $420.00

Ruger Model 77 Mark NV (Varmint)
Similar to the Model Mark II R except: calibers: 22-250, 220 Swift, 25-06, 223, 243, or 308; laminated wood stock; 26" barrel
Estimated Value: $340.00 - $430.00

Ruger Model 77 Mark IIRSM, IIVRSM
Caliber: 375 H&H, 416 Rigby, or 458 Win. magnum (1992)
Action: Bolt action; repeating; stainless steel bolt; three position swing-back safety
Magazine: 4-shot (375 H&H); 3-shot (416 Rigby or 458 Win.); floor plate latch is housed in the trigger guard
Barrel: 24"; blued, with sighting plane of cross serrations to reduce glare
Stock & Forearm: Checkered walnut, one-piece pistol grip stock & forearm
Estimated Value: $930.00 - $1,160.00

Ruger Mini 14
Caliber: 223 Commercial or Military
Action: Semi-automatic, gas operated
Magazine: 5-shot detachable box; 10 & 20-shot available
Barrel: 18½"; blued or stainless steel; add 10% for stainless steel
Stock & Forearm: Plain walnut, semi-pistol grip, one piece stock & forearm; hand guard over barrel; folding stock & pistol grip available after mid 1980's
Estimated Value: $295.00 - $370.00

Ruger Mini 14/5-R, Ranch Rifle
Similar to the Mini 14 except: internal improvements & integral scope mounts; add 9.5% for stainless steel
Estimated Value: $320.00 - $395.00

Ruger Model 77RLS
Caliber: 270 or 30-06,
Action: Bolt action; repeating; long action
Magazine: 5-shot box with hinged floor plates; 4-shot in magnum
Barrel: 18½"
Stock & Forearm: Checkered pistol grip, one-piece stock & tapered forearm; rubber recoil pad; swivels
Estimated Value: $350.00 - $440.00

Ruger Mini Thirty
Caliber: 7.62x39mm
Action: Semi-automatic, gas operated
Magazine: 5-shot detachable staggered box
Barrel: 18½"; blued or stainless steel
Stock & Forearm: Plain walnut, pistol grip one-piece stock & forearm with hand guard; add 9% for stainless steel
Estimated Value: $320.00 - $395.00

Ruger Model XGI
Caliber: 243 or 308
Action: Gas operated, semi-automatic, based on the Garand system used in the U.S. M1 & M14 military rifles
Magazine: 5-shot staggered column, detachable box
Barrel: 20"; blued with hanguard cover
Stock & Forearm: Plain one-piece American hardwood, reinforced with steel liners
Estimated Value: $300.00 - $375.00

Ruger

Ruger Model 10/22

Ruger Model 10/22 Sporter

Ruger Model 10/22 International

Ruger Model 10/22
Caliber: 22 long rifle
Action: Semi-automatic
Magazine: 10-shot detachable rotary
Barrel: 18½"; blued
Stock & Forearm: Plain hardwood one-piece semi-pistol grip stock & forearm; barrel band; add 18% for stainless steel
Estimated Value: $115.00 - $145.00

Ruger Model 10/22, Deluxe Sporter
Similar to the Model 10/22 with Monte Carlo or regular checkered walnut stock; fluted bandless forearm; swivels
Estimated Value: $150.00 - $190.00

Ruger Model 10/22, International
Similar to Model 10/22 except: full-length forearm; swivels
Estimated Value: $140.00 - $175.00

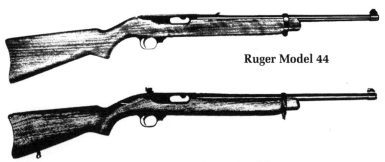

Ruger Model 44

Ruger Model 44 RS Deluxe

Ruger Model 44 RS Deluxe
Similar to Model 44 with peep sight & swivels
Estimated Value: $255.00 - $325.00

Ruger Model 44
Caliber: 44 magnum
Action: Semi-auto, gas operated
Magazine: 4-shot tubular
Barrel: 18½"; blued
Stock & Forearm: Plain walnut one-piece semi-pistol grip stock & forearm; barrel band
Estimated Value: $250.00 - $320.00

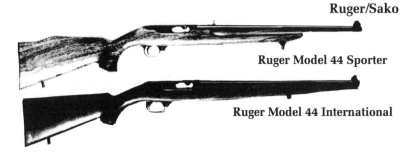

Ruger Model 44 Sporter

Ruger Model 44 International

Ruger Model 44 International
Similar to Model 44 except: full-length forearm & swivels
Estimated Value: $300.00 - $375.00

Ruger Model 44 Sporter
Similar to Model 44 except: Monte Carlo stock; fluted forearm & swivels
Estimated Value: $270.00 - $340.00

Sako

Sako Vixen Sporter

Sako Finsport 2700

Sako Vixen Mannlicher

Sako Finsport 2700
Caliber: 270 Win., 30-06, 7mm Rem. mag., or 338 Win. mag.
Action: Long throw bolt action; adjustable trigger
Magazine: 5-shot
Barrel: 23½"; blued
Stock & Forearm: Checkered walnut, Monte Carlo pistol grip, one-piece stock & forearm; recoil pad; swivels
Estimated Value: $560.00 - $700.00

Sako Vixen Sporter
Caliber: 218 Bee, 22 Hornet, 222, or 223
Action: Bolt action, short stroke, Mauser-type
Magazine: 5-shot
Barrel: 23½"; blued
Stock & Forearm: Checkered walnut, Monte Carlo pistol grip, one-piece stock & forearm; swivels
Estimated Value: $460.00 - $575.00

Sako Vixen Mannlicher
Similar to the Sporter except: a full-length forearm; 20" barrel; barrel band
Estimated Value: $475.00 - $595.00

Sako

Sako Vixen Heavy Barrel

Sako Forester Sporter

Sako Forester Mannlicher

Sako Finnbear

Sako Finnbear Mannlicher

Sako Vixen Heavy Barrel
Similar to Vixen Sporter except:
heavy barrel & in larger calibers
Estimated Value: $480.00 - $600.00

Sako Forester Sporter
Similar to Vixen Sporter except:
medium action; 22-250, 243 or 308
calibers
Estimated Value: $490.00 - $615.00

Sako Forester Mannlicher
Similar to Forester Sporter except:
full-length forearm; 20" barrel; barrel
band
Estimated Value: $495.00 - $620.00

Sako Forester Heavy Barrel
Similar to Forester Sporter except:
heavy 24" barrel
Estimated Value: $500.00 - $625.00

Sako Finnbear
Similar to Vixen Sporter except: long
action; recoil pad; 25-06, 264
magnum, 270, 30-06, 300 magnum,
7mm magnum, or 375 H&H
Estimated Value: $505.00 - $630.00

Sako Finnbear Mannlicher
Similar to Finnbear except: full-
length stock; 20" barrel; barrel band
Estimated Value: $510.00 - $635.00

Sako Model 74 Super Sporter

Sako Model 74 Super Sporter Heavy Barrel
Similar to Model 74 Super Sporter in short, medium, or long action; heavy barrel
Estimated Value: $475.00 - $595.00

Sako Model 74 Deluxe Sporter
Similar to Model 74 Super Sporter except: recoil pad; select wood & high-quality finish; add $25.00 for magnum
Estimated Value: $495.00 - $620.00

Sako Model 74 Super Sporter
Similar to Vixen, Forester & Finnbear except: short action, medium action, or long action; 23" or 24" barrel
Estimated Value: $460.00 - $575.00

Sako Mauser

Sako Mauser
Caliber: 270 or 30-06
Action: FN Mauser bolt action; repeating
Magazine: 5-shot box
Barrel: 24"; blued
Stock & Forearm: Checkered walnut Monte Carlo one-piece pistol grip stock & tapered forearm; swivels
Estimated Value: $440.00 - $550.00

Sako Mauser Magnum
Similar to Sako Mauser except: magnum calibers 300 H&H or 375 H&H; recoil pad
Estimated Value: $480.00 - $600.00

Sako Model A1 Standard, Hunter
Caliber: 17 Rem., 222 Rem., or 223 Rem.
Action: Bolt action; repeating; short-throw bolt
Magazine: 5-shot
Barrel: 23½"
Stock & Forearm: Checkered walnut Monte Carlo one-piece pistol grip stock & forearm; lacquer or oil finish; laminated grain & fiberglass available in 1989; swivels; add 4% for 17 Rem. caliber; add 20% for laminated stock & 30% for fiberglass stock
Estimated Value: $585.00 - $730.00

Sako Model A11 Standard, Hunter
Similar to the A1 Standard except: medium throw action; 220 Swift, 22-250 Rem., 243 Win., 7mm-08, or 308 Win. calibers; add 12% for laminated stock and 30% for fiberglass stock
Estimated Value: $585.00 - $730.00

Sako

Sako Model A1 Deluxe

Sako Model A1 Deluxe
A deluxe version of the A1; recoil pad
Estimated Value: $795.00 - $995.00

Sako Model A111 Standard, Hunter
Similar to the Model A1 Standard with a long throw action; 25-06 Rem., 6.5x55, 270 Win., 280 Rem., 7x64, 30-06, 7mm Rem. mag., 300 Win. mag., 338 Win. mag., 9.3x62, or 375 H&H mag.; recoil pad; add $25.00 - $40.00 for mag; add 12% for laminated stock & 30% for fiberglass stock
Estimated Value: $600.00 - $750.00

Sako Model A11 Deluxe
Similar to the Model A11 except: deluxe features; recoil pad
Estimated Value: $795.00 - $995.00

Sako Model A111 Deluxe
Similar to the Model A111 except: deluxe features; add $25.00 for magnum
Estimated Value: $820.00 - $1,025.00

Sako Varmint

Sako Varmint
Similar to the Models A1, A11 & A111 except: heavy varmint barrel
Estimated Value: $665.00 - $835.00

Sako Carbine, Mannlicher
Similar to the Models A1, A11, & A111 except: 20" barrel; full-length forearm; add 6% for 375 H&H & 3% for other magnums
Estimated Value: $675.00 - $850.00

Sako Safari Grade

Sako Classic Grade
Similar to the A111 & A11 except: styling changes; 243 Win., 270 Win., 30-06, or 7mm Rem. magnum; select American walnut stock
Estimated Value: $535.00 - $730.00

Sako Safari Grade
Similar to the A111 except: extended magazine; barrel band swivels, select French walnut stock; choice of satin or matte blue finish; calibers 300 Win. magnum, 338 Win. magnum, or 375 H&H magnum
Estimated Value: $1,575.00 - $1,965.00

Sako Finnwolf Sporter

Sako Model 78
Caliber: 22 long rifle, 22 Win. magnum, or 22 Hornet; add 5% for 22 Hornet
Action: Bolt action; repeating
Magazine: 5-shot; 4-shot in magnum
Barrel: 22½"; regular or heavy barrel
Stock & Forearm: One-piece checkered walnut Monte Carlo pistol grip stock & forearm; swivels
Estimated Value: $415.00 - $520.00

Sako Finnwolf Sporter
Caliber: 243 or 308
Action: Lever-action; hammerless; repeating
Magazine: 4-shot clip
Barrel: 23"; blued
Stock & Forearm: Checkered walnut Monte Carlo one-piece pistol grip stock and tapered forearm; swivels
Estimated Value: $460.00 - $575.00

Sako Finnwolf Deluxe Sporter
Same as Finnwolf Sporter except: select wood
Estimated Value: $500.00 - $625.00

Savage

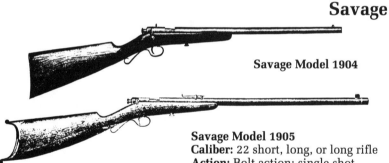

Savage Model 1904

Savage Model 1911 Target

Savage Model 1904 & Model 04
Caliber: 22 short, long, or long rifle
Action: Bolt action; single shot
Magazine: None; single-shot
Barrel: 18"
Stock & Forearm: Straight wood one-piece stock & forearm; a boy's lightweight takedown rifle produced from 1904 to 1917 as Model 1904 & from 1924 to 1930 as Model 04
Estimated Value: $80.00 - $100.00

Savage Model 1905
Caliber: 22 short, long, or long rifle
Action: Bolt action; single shot
Magazine: None; single-shot
Barrel: 22"
Stock & Forearm: Plain one-piece straight grip stock & forearm; a lightweight takedown boy's rifle
Estimated Value: $85.00 - $110.00

Savage Model 1911 Target
Caliber: 22 short
Action: Bolt action; single shot
Magazine: None; single-shot
Barrel: 20"
Stock & Forearm: Walnut one-piece straight grip stock & forearm
Estimated Value: $100.00 - $125.00

Savage

Savage Model 19

Savage Model 19 & 19L Target
Caliber: 22 long rifle
Action: Bolt action; repeating; speed lock
Magazine: 5-shot detachable box
Barrel: 25"
Stock & Forearm: Walnut pistol grip stock & beavertail forearm; swivels; Model 19L has special Lyman receiver & front sights
Estimated Value: $150.00 - $200.00

Savage Model 19M
Same as the Model 19 except: heavier 28" barrel
Estimated Value: $185.00 - $230.00

Savage Model 19H Hornet
Same as Model 19 except: loading port, bolt mechanism & magazine are like Model 23-D; 22 Hornet caliber only
Estimated Value: $240.00 - $300.00

Savage Model 19 NRA

Savage Model 20

Savage Model 19 NRA Match Rifle
Caliber: 22 long rifle
Action: Bolt action; repeating
Magazine: 5-shot detachable box
Barrel: 25"
Stock & Forearm: Full military pistol grip wood stock & forearm
Estimated Value: $195.00 - $245.00

Savage Model 20
Caliber: 300 Savage or 250-3000
Action: Bolt action; repeating
Magazine: 5-shot
Barrel: 22" in 250 caliber; 24" in 300 caliber
Stock & Forearm: Checkered walnut pistol grip stock & forearm
Estimated Value: $260.00 - $330.00

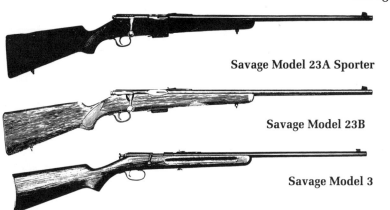

Savage Model 23A Sporter

Savage Model 23B

Savage Model 3

Savage Model 3, 3S, 3ST
Caliber: 22 short, long, or long rifle
Action: Bolt action; single shot
Magazine: None; single-shot
Barrel: 26" before World War II; 24" after
Stock & Forearm: One-piece walnut semi-pistol grip stock & forearm; 3ST has swivels
Estimated Value: $90.00 - $110.00

Savage Model 23A Sporter, 23AA, 23B, 23C, 23D
Caliber: 22 long rifle (Model 23A, 23AA), 22 Hornet (Model 23 D); 25-20 (Model 23B); 32-20 (Model 23C)
Action: Bolt action; (Model 23AA, speed lock)
Magazine: 5-shot detachable box
Barrel: 23"or 25"
Stock & Forearm: Plain walnut semi-pistol grip stock & forearm
Estimated Value: $180.00 - $225.00

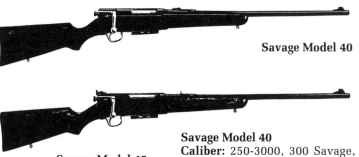

Savage Model 40

Savage Model 45

Savage Model 45
This is a special grade version of the Model 40. It has a checkered stock & forearm.
Estimated Value: $255.00 - $320.00

Savage Model 40
Caliber: 250-3000, 300 Savage, 30-30, or 30-06
Action: Bolt action; repeating
Magazine: 4-shot detachable box
Barrel: 22" for caliber 250-3000 or 30-30; 24" for other calibers
Stock & Forearm: Plain or checkered walnut pistol grip stock & lipped or plain forearm
Estimated Value: $225.00 - $285.00

Savage

Savage Model 4

Savage Model 4S

Savage Model 4M

Savage Model 5

Savage Model 5S

Savage Model 5 & 5S
Similar to the Model 4 except: tubular magazine; Model 5S has peep rear & hooded front sight. Produced from the mid 1930's until 1961 in caliber 22 short, long & long rifle
Estimated Value: $95.00 - $120.00

Savage Model 4, 4S, & 4M
Caliber: 22 short, long, or long rifle; 4M chambered for 22 mag.
Action: Bolt action; repeating
Magazine: 5-shot detachable box
Barrel: 24"
Stock & Forearm: Checkered walnut pistol grip stock & grooved forearm on pre-World War II models; plain on post-World War II models
Estimated Value: $85.00 - $110.00

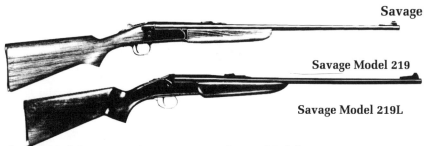

Savage Model 219

Savage Model 219L

Savage Model 219 & 219L
Caliber: 22 Hornet, 25-20, 32-20, or 30-30
Action: Hammerless; single shot; automatic ejector; shotgun style, top break; 219L has side lever break
Magazine: none; single-shot
Barrel: 26"
Stock & Forearm: Plain walnut pistol grip stock & forearm
Estimated Value: $75.00 - $100.00

Savage Model 221 Utility Gun
Same rifle as the Model 219 except: 30-30 only with an interchangeable 12 gauge 30" shotgun barrel; priced to include the 12 gauge interchangeable shotgun barrel
Estimated Value: $105.00 - $130.00

Savage Model 222
Same as Model 221 except: shotgun barrel is 16 gauge; 28"
Estimated Value: $105.00 - $130.00

Savage Model 223
Same as Model 221 except: shotgun barrel is 20 gauge; 28"
Estimated Value: $105.00 - $130.00

Savage Model 227
Same as Model 221 except: 22 Hornet; the shotgun barrel is 12 gauge; 30"
Estimated Value: $110.00 - $135.00

Savage Model 228
Same as Model 227 except: shotgun barrel is 16 gauge; 28"
Estimated Value: $110.00 - $135.00

Savage Model 229
Same as Model 227 except: shotgun barrel is 20 gauge; 28"
Estimated Value: $110.00 - $135.00

Savage Model 110 Sporter

Savage Model 110 MC & MCL
Same as 110 Sporter except: 22-250 caliber; 24" barrel; Monte Carlo stock. The MCL is the same in left-hand action
Estimated Value: $180.00 - $225.00

Savage Model 110 Sporter
Caliber: 243, 270, 308, or 30-06
Action: Bolt action; repeating
Magazine: 4-shot staggered box
Barrel: 22"
Stock & Forearm: Checkered walnut pistol grip stock & forearm
Estimated Value: $150.00 - $200.00

Savage

Savage Model 110E

Savage Model 112-R

Savage Model 110 M

Savage Model 110E, 110EL (Early)
Caliber: 243 Win., 7mm Rem. mag., or 30-06
Action: Bolt action; repeating
Magazine: 4-shot staggered box; 3-shot in magnum
Barrel: 20"; blued; stainless steel in magnum
Stock & Forearm: One-piece checkered or plain walnut Monte Carlo stock & forearm; magnum has recoil pad; 110EL is a left hand model
Estimated Value: $170.00 - $225.00

Savage Model 110 M & 110 ML
Caliber: 7mm Rem. mag., 264, 300, or 338 Win.
Action: Bolt action; repeating
Magazine: 4-shot box, staggered
Barrel: 24"
Stock & Forearm: Walnut Monte Carlo pistol grip stock & forearm; recoil pad; 110ML is left hand model
Estimated Value: $190.00 - $250.00

Savage Model 110C, 110CL
Caliber: 22-250, 243, 25-06, 270, 308, 30-06, 7mm Rem. mag., or 300 Win. mag.
Action: Bolt action; repeating
Magazine: 4-shot clip, 3-shot clip in magnum calibers
Barrel: 22" or 24"
Stock & Forearm: Checkered walnut Monte Carlo stock & forearm; magnum has recoil pad; add 10% for magnum calibers; 110CL is left hand model
Estimated Value: $225.00 - $300.00

Savage Model 110S
Similar to the Model 110C except: heavy barrel; no sights; stippled checkering; recoil pad; 7mm/08 or 308 calibers
Estimated Value: $260.00 - $325.00

Savage Model 112-R
A varmint rifle similar to the Model 110C except: plain walnut one-piece semi-pistol grip stock & forearm; swivels; recoil pad; 22-250 or 25-06 calibers
Estimated Value: $205.00 - $260.00

Savage Model 110P

Savage Model 110-D & 110-DL
Caliber: 223, 243, 270, 30-06, 7mm Rem. magnum, or 338 Win. magnum
Action: Bolt action; repeating
Magazine: 4-shot internal box; 3-shot for magnums
Barrel: 22"; blue; 24" for magnums
Stock & Forearm: Select walnut, checkered semi-pistol grip, Monte Carlo, one-piece stock & forearm; add 18% for magnum calibers; 110-DL is left hand model
Estimated Value: $210.00 - $275.00

Savage Model 110E & 110G
Caliber: 22-250, 223, 243, 308 Win., 270, 30-06, 7mm Rem. mag., or 300 Win. mag.
Action: Bolt action; repeating
Magazine: 4-shot box, internal
Barrel: 22" or 24"; blued
Stock & Forearm: Checkered hardwood, Monte Carlo walnut finish, one-piece pistol grip stock & forearm
Estimated Value: $225.00 - $285.00

Savage Model 110FP Police Rifle
Similar to the Model 110G except: 223 Remington or 308 Winchester caliber only; heavy, 24" barrel; non-reflective black finish on metal parts; black all-weather DuPont Rynite® one-piece stock & forearm; sling studs & bi-pod mount; no sights; drilled & tapped for scope mounts
Estimated Value: $265.00 - $330.00

Savage Model 110V & 110GV
Similar to Model 110E & 110G except: 22-250 or 223 caliber; heavy 26" barrel; recoil pad
Estimated Value: $245.00 - $310.00

Savage Model 110P Premier & 110 PL
Caliber: 243 Win., 7mm Rem. mag., or 30-06
Action: Bolt action; repeating
Magazine: 4-shot box, staggered; 3-shot in magnum
Barrel: 22"or 24"; blued; stainless steel in magnum
Stock & Forearm: Walnut & rosewood Monte Carlo stock & forearm; swivels; magnum has recoil pad; 110PL is left-hand action; add $15.00 for magnum
Estimated Value: $310.00 - $390.00

Savage 110PE Presentation, 110PEL
Same as Models 110P & 110PL except: receiver, floor plate & trigger guard are engraved; it was produced for two years beginning in 1968; add $15.00 for magnum; 110 PEL is left hand action
Estimated Value: $480.00 - $600.00

Savage Model 110F
Same as the Model 110G except: black DuPont Rynite® stock & forearm; add 4% for sights
Estimated Value: $245.00 - $305.00

Savage Model 110B
Same as the Model 110G except: brown laminate hardwood stock
Estimated Value: $260.00 - $325.00

Savage

Savage Model 111
Caliber: 7mm (7x57), 243, 270, 30-06, or 7mm magnum
Action: Bolt action; repeating
Magazine: 4-shot box; 3-shot box in magnum
Barrel: 24"
Stock & Forearm: Checkered walnut Monte Carlo one-piece pistol grip stock & forearm; swivels; add $10.00 for magnum
Estimated Value: $220.00 - $275.00

Savage Model 112V
Caliber: 222, 223, 22-250, 220 Swift, 25-06, or 243
Action: Bolt action; single shot; hammerless
Magazine: None; single-shot
Barrel: 26"; chrome-moly steel; tapered
Stock & Forearm: Checkered walnut one-piece pistol grip stock & forearm; fluted comb; swivels
Estimated Value: $205.00 - $260.00

Savage Model 111

Savage Model 112V

Savage Model 340

Savage Model 340C Carbine

Savage Model 340S
Same as Model 340 except: peep rear & hooded front sights
Estimated Value: $135.00 - $185.00

Savage Model 340C Carbine
Same as Model 340 except: caliber 30-30; the barrel is slightly over 18"; checkered stock & sling swivels
Estimated Value: $135.00 - $180.00

Savage Model 340
Caliber: 22 Hornet, 222 Rem., 223 Rem., or 30-30
Action: Bolt action; repeating
Magazine: 4-shot clip in 22 Hornet & 222 Rem.; 3-shot clip in 30-30
Barrel: 20", 22", or 24"
Stock & Forearm: Plain walnut pistol grip stock & forearm; checkered after 1965; before 1950 it was manufactured as a Stevens
Estimated Value: $130.00 - $175.00

Savage Fox Model FB-1

Savage Model 65-M

Savage Model 65-M
Caliber: 22 magnum
Action: Bolt action; repeating
Magazine: 5-shot clip
Barrel: 22"; blued
Stock & Forearm: Checkered walnut
one-piece semi-pistol grip stock &
forearm
Estimated Value: $75.00 - $90.00

Savage Fox Model FB-1
Caliber: 22 short, long, or long rifle
Action: Bolt action; repeating
Magazine: 5-shot detachable clip
Barrel: 24"; blued
Stock & Forearm: Checkered walnut
Monte Carlo one-piece semi-pistol
grip stock & forearm; cheekpiece;
swivels; rosewood fore-end tip &
grip cap
Estimated Value: $150.00 - $200.00

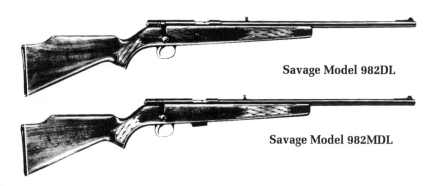

Savage Model 982DL

Savage Model 982MDL

Savage Model 982MDL
Caliber: 22 magnum
Action: Bolt action; repeating
Magazine: 5-shot detachable clip
Barrel: 22"; blued
Stock & Forearm: Checkered walnut
Monte Carlo one-piece semi-pistol
grip stock & forearm
Estimated Value: $90.00 - $110.00

Savage Model 982DL
Caliber: 22 short, long, or long rifle
Action: Bolt action; repeating
Magazine: 5-shot clip, push button
release
Barrel: 22"; blued
Stock & Forearm: Checkered walnut
one-piece Monte Carlo semi-pistol
grip stock & forearm
Estimated Value: $80.00 - $100.00

Savage

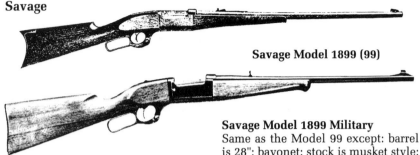

Savage Model 1899 (99)

Savage Model 99A

Savage Model 1899 Military
Same as the Model 99 except: barrel is 28"; bayonet; stock is musket style; sights are military; caliber 30-30 Win.
Estimated Value: $480.00 - $600.00

Savage Model 1899 (99)
Caliber: 303 Savage, 25-35, 32-40, 38-55, or 30-30
Action: Lever-action; hammerless
Magazine: 5-shot rotary
Barrel: 20", 22", or 26"; round, half octagon, or octagon
Stock & Forearm: Walnut straight grip stock & tapered forearm
Estimated Value: $400.00 - $500.00

Savage Model 99A
Basically the same as Model 1899 except: solid frame; in calibers 300 Savage, 303 Savage, or 30-30; produced from 1922 to 1937; later models in calibers 243, 308, 250 Savage, & 300 Savage from about 1970 to 1984; add $20.00 for early models
Estimated Value: $240.00 - $300.00

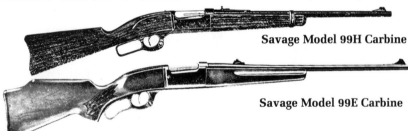

Savage Model 99H Carbine

Savage Model 99E Carbine

Savage Model 99E
Similar to the Model 99A except: 22 Hi Power, 250-3000, 30-30, 300 savage, or 303 Savage; 22" or 24" barrel; unlipped tapered forearm
Estimated Value: $320.00 - $400.00

Savage Model 99H Carbine
Basically the same as 99A except: addition of 250-3000 caliber; short barrel; carbine stock & forearm; barrel bands
Estimated Value: $330.00 - $410.00

Savage Model 99B
Takedown version of Model 99A
Estimated Value: $340.00 - $425.00

Savage Model 99E Carbine
Similar to the Model 99H except: 243 Win., 250 Savage, 300 Savage, or 308 Win., calibers only; checkered walnut stock & tapered forearm without barrel band; production began in 1961; Monte Carlo stock after 1982
Estimated Value: $195.00 - $260.00

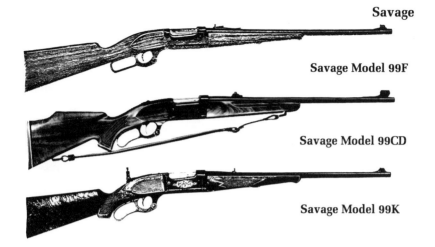

Savage Model 99F

Savage Model 99CD

Savage Model 99K

Savage Model 99EG II
Similar to the Model G except: produced after World War II from 1946 to 1961
Estimated Value: $220.00 - $275.00

Savage Model 99CD
A solid frame version of Model 99F with a checkered pistol grip stock & forearm; in production from 1955 to about 1980; 4-shot detachable box magazine
Estimated Value: $225.00 - $285.00

Savage Model 99G
A takedown version of the Model 99E with a checkered walnut pistol grip stock & forearm; made from about 1921 to 1941
Estimated Value: $335.00 - $420.00

Savage Model 99K
A fancy Model 99G with deluxe stock & light engraving; rear sight is peep, & there is a folding middle sight; made from the early 1930's to the early 1940's
Estimated Value: $780.00 - $975.00

Savage Model 99F
This is a lightweight takedown version of the Model 99E, produced until about 1940; production resumed about 1955 to 1972 in caliber 243, 300, & 308; add $160.00 for pre-1940
Estimated Value: $220.00 - $275.00

Savage Model 99R II
Similar to other Model 99's; production stopped in 1940; it was resumed from 1946 to 1961 in 24" barrel only with swivel attachments in a variety of calibers; add $150.00 for pre-World War II models
Estimated Value: $240.00 - $300.00

Savage Model 99RS I (Pre-WWII) 99RSII (Postwar)
The same rifle as Model 99 except those before World War II have rear peep sight & folding middle sight. Those made after the war have a special receiver sight. Discontinued in 1961; solid frame; add $160.00 for pre-World War II models
Estimated Value: $240.00 - $300.00

Savage

Savage Model 99DL

Savage Model 99PE Presentation

Savage Model 99C

Savage Model 99T

Savage Model 99PE Presentation
Similar to the Model 99DL except: engraved receiver; hand checkered Monte Carlo stock & forearm; produced from 1968 to 1970
Estimated Value: $600.00 - $750.00

Savage Model 99DE Citation
A less elaborate example of the Model 99 PE; produced from 1968 to 1970
Estimated Value: $440.00 - $550.00

Savage Model 99T
Basically the same as the other Model 99's; it is a solid frame with a checkered walnut pistol grip stock & forearm; produced until 1940
Estimated Value: $290.00 - $360.00

Savage Model 99C
Caliber: 22-250, 243, 308, or 7mm/08
Action: Hammerless lever action; cocking indicator
Magazine: 3 or 4-shot detachable clip
Barrel: 22"; chrome-moly steel
Stock & Forearm: Checkered walnut semi-pistol grip, two-piece stock, & tapered forearm; Monte Carlo stock after 1982
Estimated Value: $305.00 - $385.00

Savage Model 99DL
This is a late Model 99; in production from about 1960 to mid 1970's; basically the same as Model 99F with a Monte Carlo stock & swivels
Estimated Value: $215.00 - $270.00

Pocket Guide to Rifles

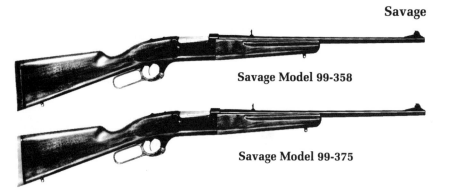

Savage Model 99-358

Savage Model 99-375

Savage Model 99-375
Similar to the Model 99-358 except:
375 Win. caliber
Estimated Value: $240.00 - $300.00

Savage Model 99-358
Similar to the Model 99A except:
358 caliber; forearm rounded;
swivels; recoil pad; made from late
1970's to early 1980's
Estimated Value: $235.00 - $295.00

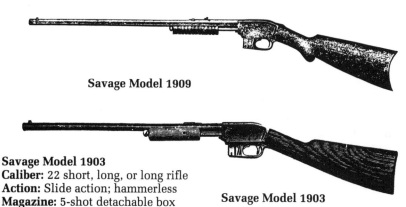

Savage Model 1909

Savage Model 1903

Savage Model 1903
Caliber: 22 short, long, or long rifle
Action: Slide action; hammerless
Magazine: 5-shot detachable box
Barrel: 24"; octagon
Stock & Forearm: Checkered walnut
pistol grip stock & grooved slide
handle
Estimated Value: $170.00 - $210.00

Savage Model 1909
A lighter version of the Model 1903
with a straight stock & forearm;
round 20" barrel; discontinued about
1915
Estimated Value: $160.00 - $200.00

Savage Model 1914
Caliber: 22 short, long, or long rifle
Action: Slide action; hammerless
Magazine: Tubular; 20 shorts, 17
longs, or 15 long rifle
Barrel: 24"; octagon or half octagon
Stock & Forearm: Plain wood pistol
grip stock & grooved slide handle
Estimated Value: $155.00 - $195.00

Savage

Savage Model 25

Savage Model 29
Similar to the Model 25 except: prewar models were checkered; barrel is round on postwar models; made from 1929 until the late 1960's; add $50.00 for pre-World War II models with octagon barrel
Estimated Value: $160.00 - $200.00

Savage Model 25
Caliber: 22 short, long, or long rifle
Action: Slide action; hammerless
Magazine: Tubular; 20 shorts, 17 longs, or 15 long rifle
Barrel: 24"; octagon
Stock & Forearm: Walnut pistol grip stock & grooved slide handle
Estimated Value: $170.00 - $220.00

Savage Model 170-C

Savage Model 1912
Caliber: 22 long rifle
Action: Semi-automatic; hammerless
Magazine: 7-shot detachable box
Barrel: 20"; half octagon
Stock & Forearm: Plain wood straight grip stock & forearm; savage's first semi-automatic; discontinued in 1916
Estimated Value: $210.00 - $275.00

Savage Model 170
Caliber: 30-30 or 35
Action: Slide action; hammerless; repeating
Magazine: 3-shot tubular
Barrel: 22"; blued
Stock & Forearm: Checkered walnut Monte Carlo semi-pistol grip stock & fluted slide handle; swivels
Estimated Value: $140.00 - $175.00

Savage Model 170-C
A carbine version of the Model 170; plain stock; 18½" barrel; 30-30 caliber only
Estimated Value: $130.00 - $165.00

Savage Model 6

Savage Model 7 & 7S
Basically the same as Model 6 & 6S except: 5-shot detachable box magazine; produced from the late 1930's until the early 1950's.
Estimated Value: $80.00 - $100.00

Savage Model 6, 6S
Caliber: 22 short, long, or long rifle
Action: Semi-automatic
Magazine: Tubular; 21 shorts, 17 longs, or 15 long rifle
Barrel: 24"
Stock & Forearm: Checkered walnut pistol grip before World War II; plain walnut pistol grip after the war
Estimated Value: $95.00 - $120.00

Savage Model 80

Savage Model 980DL
Caliber: 22 long rifle
Action: Semi-automatic
Magazine: 15-shot tubular
Barrel: 20"; blued
Stock & Forearm: Checkered walnut one-piece Monte Carlo semi-pistol grip stock and forearm
Estimated Value: $95.00 - $120.00

Savage Model 80
Caliber: 22 long rifle
Action: Semi-automatic
Magazine: 15-shot tubular
Barrel: 20"; blued
Stock & Forearm: Checkered walnut one-piece Monte Carlo pistol grip stock & forearm
Estimated Value: $80.00 - $100.00

Stevens

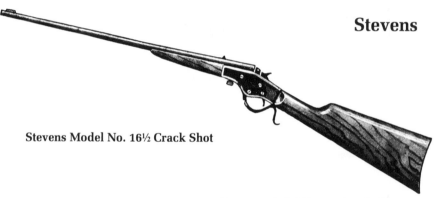

Stevens Model No. 16½ Crack Shot

Stevens Model No. 14 Little Scout
Caliber: 22 long rifle
Action: Pivoted block; exposed hammer; single shot
Magazine: None; single-shot
Barrel: 18"; round
Stock & Forearm: Plain walnut one-piece straight grip stock & forearm
Estimated Value: $120.00 - $160.00

Stevens Model No. 14½
Little Scout
Similar to the Model No. 14 Little scout except: rolling block action & separated, short forearm; produced from 1912 to World War II
Estimated Value: $115.00 - $150.00

Stevens Model No. 16 Crack Shot
Caliber: 22 long rifle or 32 short
Action: Falling block; single shot; exposed hammer; lever action
Magazine: None; single-shot
Barrel: 20"; round
Stock & Forearm: Plain walnut straight grip stock with slightly lipped forearm; produced from the turn of the century until 1912
Estimated Value: $200.00 - $250.00

Stevens Model No. 16½
Crack Shot
Same as No. 16 except: smooth bore for shot cartridges; produced from 1907 to 1912
Estimated Value: $190.00 - $240.00

Stevens

Stevens Tip Up Model No. 2

Stevens Model No. 15 Maynard Jr.
Caliber: 22 long rifle or short
Action: Lever action; tip up; exposed hammer
Magazine: None; single-shot
Barrel: 18"; part octagon
Stock & Forearm: Plain walnut, straight stock & short forearm; this small rifle was made to compete with cheap imports; produced from 1901 to 1910
Estimated Value: $110.00 - $140.00

Stevens Model No. 15½ Maynard Jr.
Same as the No. 15 Maynard Jr. except: smooth bore for 22 long rifle shot cartridges
Estimated Value: $100.00 - $135.00

Stevens Tip Up Model No. 2

Stevens Tip Up Models No. 2, 5, 6, 7, 8, 9, 11 & 13 Ladies
Caliber: RF 22 long rifles, 25 Stevens, or 32 long (#11)
Action: Single shot, tip up; exposed hammer
Magazine: None; single-shot
Barrel: 24" octagon for #2; 28" half octagon optional on #7, all others 24" half octagon
Stock & Forearm: Walnut straight stock & forearm; no forearm on #2 or #5; this series was replaced in 1902 by a line of falling block rifles.
Estimated Value: $190.00 - $250.00

Stevens Tip Up Model No. 17 & 27 Favorite
Caliber: 22 long rifle, 25RF, or 32RF
Action: Lever action; single shot; exposed hammer
Magazine: None; single-shot
Barrel: 24"; round (octagon barrel on Model 27); other lengths available as option
Stock & Forearm: Plain walnut straight grip stock, short tapered forearm; takedown model was produced from the 1890's until the mid 1930's.
Estimated Value: $130.00 - $165.00

Stevens Model No. 17 Favorite

Stevens Model No. 18 & 28 Favorite
Same as Model No. 17 except: a Beach combination front sight, Vernier peep rear sight & leaf middle sight; Model 28 has octagon barrel
Estimated Value: $155.00 - $195.00

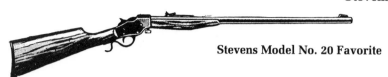

Stevens Model No. 20 Favorite

Stevens Model No. 20 Favorite
Same as the Model No. 17 except:
barrel is smooth bore for 22 RF & 32
RF shot cartridges
Estimated Value: $145.00 - $180.00

Stevens Model No. 19 & 29 Favorite
Same as the Model No. 17 except:
Lyman front sight, leaf middle sight
& Lyman combination rear sight;
Model 29 has octagon barrel
Estimated Value: $160.00 - $200.00

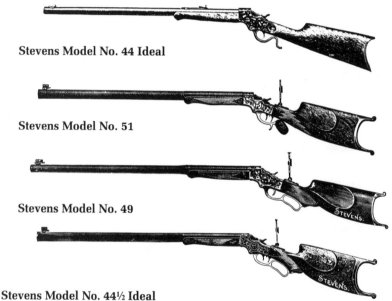

Stevens Model No. 44 Ideal

Stevens Model No. 51

Stevens Model No. 49

Stevens Model No. 44½ Ideal
Same as the Model 44 except: falling
block action; discontinued in 1916
Estimated Value: $360.00 - $450.00

Stevens Model No. 52

Stevens Model No. 45 to 54
These rifles are structurally the same
as the Model 44. They differ in
engraving & finishes & are generally
fancy models that bring extremely
high prices. They were produced
until World War I; target sights &
stocks
Estimated Value: $415.00 - $1,000.00

Stevens Model No. 44 Ideal
Caliber: 22 long rifle; 25 RF, 25-20
SS, 32-20, 32-40, 38-55, or 44-40
Action: Lever action; rolling block;
exposed hammer; single shot
Magazine: None; single-shot
Barrel: 24" or 26"; round, octagon, or
half-octagon
Stock & Forearm: Plain walnut,
straight grip; produced from the late
1890's until the early 1930's
Estimated Value: $310.00 - $390.00

Stevens

Stevens Model No. 425 High Power

Stevens Model No. 414 Armory
Caliber: 22 long rifle or 22 short only
Action: Lever action; exposed hammer; rolling block
Magazine: None; single-shot
Barrel: 26"; heavy round
Sights: Rocky Mountain front, adjustable receiver rear
Stock & Forearm: Plain walnut straight grip, military stock, & forearm; bands; swivels; made from 1912 until the early 1930's
Estimated Value: $260.00 - $350.00

Stevens Model No. 425 High Power
Caliber: Rimless Rem. 25, 30, 32, or 35; smokeless flatnose
Action: Lever action; exposed hammer; single extractor
Magazine: 5-shot tubular, under barrel
Barrel: 22"; round
Stock & Forearm: Plain walnut straight grip stock & forearm; made for about five years beginning in 1911
Estimated Value: $200.00 - $250.00

Stevens Model No. 12 Marksman

Stevens Model No. 26 Crack Shot
Caliber: 22 long rifle or 32 RF
Action: Lever action; exposed hammer; single shot
Magazine: None; single-shot
Barrel: 18" or 22"
Stock & Forearm: Plain walnut straight grip stock & tapered forearm; takedown rifle produced from 1913 until prior to World War II
Estimated Value: $130.00 - $165.00

Stevens Model No. 26½
Same as the No. 26 Crack shot except: smooth bore for shot cartridges
Estimated Value: $125.00 - $160.00

Stevens Model No. 26½

Stevens Model No. 12 Marksman
Caliber: 22 long rifle, 25 RF, or 32 RF
Action: Lever action; tip up; exposed hammer; single shot
Magazine: None; single shot
Barrel: 20"; round
Stock & Forearm: Plain walnut straight grip stock & short tapered forearm; made from 1912 to 1916
Estimated Value: $120.00 - $150.00

Stevens Model No. 417

Stevens Model No. 417½

Stevens Model No. 417-1

Stevens Model No. 418

Stevens Model No. 72 Crackshot

Stevens Model No. 417, 417½, 417-1, 417-2,& 417-3 Walnut Hill
Caliber: 22 long rifle; 22 WRF, or 25 Stevens
Action: Lever action; exposed hammer; single shot
Magazine: None; single-shot
Barrel: 28" or 29"; heavy
Stock & Forearm: Plain walnut pistol grip stock & forearm; bands, swivels; models differ only in sight combinations
Estimated Value: $400.00 - $500.00

Stevens Model No. 418 & 418½ Walnut Hill
Caliber: No. 418: 22 long rifle or 22 short; No. 418½: 22 WRF or 25 Stevens RF
Action: Lever action; exposed hammer; single shot
Magazine: None; single-shot
Barrel: 26"
Stock & Forearm: Plain walnut pistol grip stock & forearm; swivels; made from the early 1930's to just before World War II
Estimated Value: $320.00 - $400.00

Stevens Model No. 72 Crackshot
Caliber: 22 short, long, or long rifle
Action: Lever action; falling block; single shot
Magazine: None; single-shot
Barrel: 22"; octagon
Stock & Forearm: Plain walnut straight grip stock & tapered forearm; case hardened receiver
Estimated Value: $80.00 - $110.00

Stevens

Stevens Model No. 89

Stevens - Springfield Model No. 51 Reliance

Stevens - Springfield Model No. 52 Challenge

Stevens Model No. 65

Stevens - Springfield Model No. 51 Reliance
Caliber: 22 short, long, or long rifle
Action: Bolt action; single shot
Magazine: None; single-shot
Barrel: 20"; round
Stock & Forearm: Plain walnut one-piece straight grip stock & forearm
Estimated Value: $65.00 - $85.00

Stevens - Springfield Model No. 52 Challenge
Caliber: 22 short, long, or long rifle
Action: Bolt action; single shot
Magazine: None; single-shot
Barrel: 22"; round
Stock & Forearm: Plain walnut one-piece pistol grip stock & forearm
Estimated Value: $55.00 - $70.00

Stevens - Springfield Model No. 53 Springfield Jr.
Caliber: 22 short, long, or long rifle
Action: Bolt action; single-shot
Magazine: None; single-shot
Barrel: 24"
Stock & Forearm: Plain walnut semi-pistol grip stock & forearm
Estimated Value: $60.00 - $75.00

Stevens Model No. 89
Caliber: 22 short, long, or long rifle
Action: Lever action; exposed hammer; single-shot; automatic ejection
Magazine: None; single-shot
Barrel: 18½"
Stock & Forearm: Walnut straight grip stock & forearm with carbine band
Estimated Value: $65.00 - $80.00

Stevens Model No. 65 Little Krag
Caliber: 22 short, long, or long rifle
Action: Bolt action; single shot
Magazine: None; single-shot
Barrel: 20"; round
Stock & Forearm: Plain walnut one-piece straight grip stock & forearm; produced from 1903 until about 1910
Estimated Value: $120.00 - $150.00

Stevens Model No. 053 Buckhorn

Stevens Model No. 419 Junior Target
Caliber: 22 short, long, or long rifle
Action: Bolt action; single-shot
Magazine: None; single-shot
Barrel: 26"
Stock & Forearm: Plain walnut pistol grip stock with grooved forearm; swivels
Estimated Value: $70.00 - $90.00

Stevens Model No. 53, 053 Buckhorn
Caliber: 22 short, long, or long rifle; 22WRF; 25 Stevens RF
Action: Bolt action; single shot
Magazine: None; single-shot
Barrel: 24"
Stock & Forearm: Plain walnut pistol grip stock & forearm
Estimated Value: $80.00 - $100.00

Stevens Model No. 056 Buckhorn

Stevens Model No. 56 & 056 Buckhorn
Caliber: 22 short, long, or long rifle
Action: Bolt action; repeating
Magazine: 5-shot clip
Barrel: 24"
Stock & Forearm: Plain walnut pistol grip stock & black tipped forearm; 056 has peep sight
Estimated Value: $75.00 - $95.00

Stevens Model No. 66 Buckhorn
Caliber: 22 short, long, or long rifle
Action: Bolt action; repeating
Magazine: Tubular; 19 shorts, 15 longs, or 13 long rifle
Barrel: 24"
Stock & Forearm: Plain walnut semi-pistol grip stock & forearm
Estimated Value: $85.00 - $110.00

Stevens Model No. 066 Buckhorn
Same as the Model No. 66 Buckhorn except: hooded ramp front sight; open middle sight; receiver peep sight; made from mid 1930's until late 1940's
Estimated Value: $95.00 - $115.00

Stevens

Stevens - Springfield Model No. 82

Stevens - Springfield Model No. 83

Stevens - Springfield Model No. 84

Stevens - Springfield Model No. 86

Stevens - Springfield Model No. 086

Stevens - Springfield Model No. 82
Caliber: 22 short, long, or long rifle
Action: Bolt action; single shot
Magazine: None; single-shot
Barrel: 22"
Stock & Forearm: Plain walnut pistol grip stock, grooved forearm
Estimated Value: $65.00 - $80.00

Stevens - Springfield Model No. 83
Caliber: 22 short, long, long rifle, 22 WRF, or 25 Stevens RF
Action: Bolt action; single-shot
Magazine: None; single-shot
Barrel: 24"
Stock & Forearm: Plain walnut pistol grip stock with grooved forearm
Estimated Value: $75.00 - $90.00

Stevens - Springfield Model No. 84 & 084 (Stevens Model No. 84 after 1948)
Caliber: 22 short, long, or long rifle
Action: Bolt action; repeating
Magazine: 5-shot clip
Barrel: 24"
Stock & Forearm: Plain walnut pistol grip stock & forearm; black tip on forearm of Model 84
Estimated Value: $80.00 - $100.00

Stevens - Springfield Model No. 86, 086 (Stevens Model 86 after 1948)
Model 86 is same as Model 84 except: tubular magazine that holds 21 shorts, 17 longs, or 15 long rifle; made from mid 1930's until mid 1960's; Model 86 Stevens or 086 Stevens is same as 084 or 84 Stevens except it has tubular magazine
Estimated Value: $90.00 - $110.00

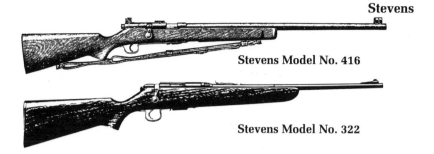

Stevens Model No. 416

Stevens Model No. 322

Stevens Model No. 416
Caliber: 22 long rifle
Action: Bolt action; repeating
Magazine: 5-shot clip
Barrel: 26"; heavy
Stock & Forearm: Plain walnut pistol grip stock & forearm
Estimated Value: $120.00 - $160.00

Stevens Model No. 322 & 322S
Caliber: 22 Hornet
Action: Bolt action; repeating
Magazine: 5-shot clip
Barrel: 21"
Stock & Forearm: Plain walnut pistol grip stock & forearm (322S has peep rear sight)
Estimated Value: $130.00 - $160.00

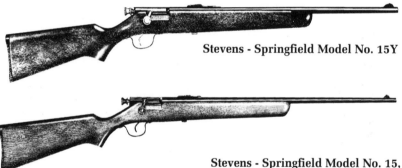

Stevens - Springfield Model No. 15Y

Stevens - Springfield Model No. 15

Stevens - Springfield Model No. 15, Stevens 15, & 15Y
Caliber: 22 short, long, or long rifle
Action: Bolt action; single-shot
Magazine: None; single-shot
Barrel: Stevens-Springfield 22"; Stevens 15, 24"; Stevens 15Y, 21"
Stock & Forearm: Plain walnut pistol grip stock and forearm; 15Y has shorter butt stock (for young shooters) & black tipped forearm; manufactured: Stevens-Springfield No. 15, late 1930's to late 1940's; Stevens 15, late 1940's to mid 1960's; Stevens 15Y, late 1950's to mid 1960's
Estimated Value: $65.00 - $80.00

Stevens Model No. 325 & 325S
Caliber: 30-30
Action: Bolt action; repeating
Magazine: 3-shot clip
Barrel: 21"
Stock & Forearm: Plain walnut pistol grip stock & forearm (325S has peep rear sight)
Estimated Value: $110.00 - $135.00

Stevens

Stevens Model No. 34

Stevens Model No. 46

Stevens Model 120
Caliber: 22 short, long, or long rifle
Action: Bolt action; single shot; pull hammer
Magazine: None; single-shot
Barrel: 24"; blued
Stock & Forearm: Plain hardwood one-piece semi-pistol grip stock & forearm
Estimated Value: $60.00 - $75.00

Stevens Model No. 34
Caliber: 22 short, long, or long rifle
Action: Bolt action; repeating
Magazine: 5-shot clip
Barrel: 20"
Stock & Forearm: Plain walnut pistol grip before 1969; checkered Monte Carlo after 1969
Estimated Value: $70.00 - $90.00

Stevens Model No 46
Similar to Model 34 except: tubular magazine; discontinued in late 1960's.
Estimated Value: $75.00 - $95.00

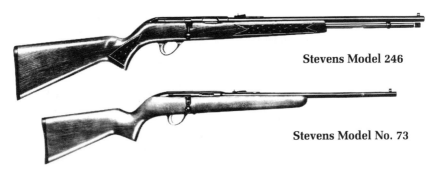

Stevens Model 246

Stevens Model No. 73

Stevens Model No. 73 & 73Y
Caliber: 22 short, long, or long rifle
Action: Bolt action; single shot
Magazine: None; single-shot
Barrel: 20" on 73; 18" on 73Y
Stock & Forearm: Plain walnut pistol grip; short stock on 73Y (for young shooters)
Estimated Value: $60.00 - $75.00

Stevens Model 246
Caliber: 22 short, long, or long rifle
Action: Bolt action; repeating
Magazine: Tubular; 22 shorts, 17 longs, or 15 long rifle
Barrel: 20"; blued
Stock & Forearm: Checkered hardwood one-piece semi-pistol grip stock & forearm
Estimated Value: $80.00 - $100.00

Stevens

Stevens Model 110E, 110ES

Stevens Model 35, 35M
Caliber: 22 short, long, or long rifle
Action: Bolt action; repeating
Magazine: 4-shot detachable clip
Barrel: 22"; blued
Stock & Forearm: Checkered hardwood Monte Carlo one-piece semi-pistol grip stock & forearm
Estimated Value: $65.00 - $85.00

Stevens Model 110E, 110ES
Caliber: 243, 30-06, or 308
Action: Bolt action; hammerless; repeating
Magazine: 4-shot box, internal
Barrel: 22"; blued
Stock & Forearm: Checkered hardwood one-piece Monte Carlo semi-pistol grip stock & forearm. Made from the late 1970's to 1981 as Stevens; merchandised after 1982 as Savage; 110ES has 4X scope; add $20.00 for 110ES
Estimated Value: $190.00 - $240.00

Stevens Model 982

Stevens Model 125
Caliber: 22 short, long, or long rifle
Action: Bolt action; single shot; pull hammer
Magazine: None; single-shot
Barrel: 22"; blued
Stock & Forearm: Checkered hardwood one-piece semi-pistol grip stock & forearm
Estimated Value: $60.00 - $75.00

Stevens Model 125Y
A youth version of the Model 125 with a shorter stock
Estimated Value: $50.00 - $65.00

Stevens Model 982
Caliber: 22 short, long, or long rifle
Action: Bolt action; repeating
Magazine: 5 or 10-shot detachable clip
Barrel: 22"; blued
Stock & Forearm: Checkered hardwood one-piece Monte Carlo semi-pistol grip stock & forearm
Estimated Value: $75.00 - $95.00

Stevens Model 36
Caliber: 22 short, long, or long rifle
Action: Bolt action; hammerless, single shot
Magazine: None; single shot
Barrel: 22"
Stock & Forearm: Hardwood, one-piece semi-pistol grip stock & forearm
Estimated Value: $65.00 - $80.00

Stevens

Stevens Model No. 70 Visible Loading

Stevens Model No. 71 Visible Loading

Stevens Model No. 80 Repeating Gallery

Stevens Model No. 75 Hammerless

Stevens Model No. 70
Visible Loading
Caliber: 22 short, long, or long rifle
Action: Slide action; exposed hammer
Magazine: Tubular; 15 shorts, 13 longs, or 11 long rifle
Barrel: 20" or 22"; round
Stock & Forearm: Plain walnut straight grip stock & grooved slide handle
Estimated Value: $175.00 - $220.00

Stevens Model No. 71 Visible Loading
Caliber: 22 short, long, or long rifle
Action: Slide action; exposed hammer
Magazine: Tubular; 15 shorts, 13 longs, 11 long rifle
Barrel: 24"; octagon
Stock & Forearm: Plain walnut pistol grip stock & grooved slide handle
Estimated Value: $170.00 - $215.00

Stevens Model No. 75 Hammerless
Caliber: 22 short, long, or long rifle
Action: Slide action; hammerless; side ejection
Magazine: Tubular; 20 shorts, 17 longs, or 15 long rifle
Barrel: 24"
Stock & Forearm: Plain walnut, straight grip stock & grooved slide handle
Estimated Value: $175.00 - $220.00

Stevens Model No. 80 Repeating Gallery
Caliber: 22 short
Action: Slide action; hammerless
Magazine: 16-shot tubular
Barrel: 24"; round
Stock & Forearm: Plain walnut straight grip stock & grooved forearm
Estimated Value: $200.00 - $250.00

Stevens - Springfield Model No. 85

Stevens - Springfield Model No. 87

Stevens Model No. 57

Stevens Model No. 76

Stevens - Springfield Model No. 85 & 085
(Stevens Model No. 85 after 1948)
Caliber: 22 long rifle
Action: Semi-automatic; repeating
Magazine: 5-shot clip
Barrel: 24"
Stock & Forearm: Plain walnut pistol grip stock & forearm; 85 has black tipped forearm. Hooded ramp front & peep rear on model 085 & 85 Stevens
Estimated Value: $90.00 - $110.00

Stevens - Springfield Model No. 87 & 087 (Stevens Model 87 after 1948)
Same as the No. 85, 085 except: 15-shot tubular magazine
Estimated Value: $95.00 - $120.00

Stevens Model No. 87 K Scout
Carbine version of Model No. 87; 20" barrel; produced until 1969.
Estimated Value: $80.00 - $100.00

Stevens Model 987 & 987T
Caliber: 22 long rifle
Action: Semi-automatic
Magazine: 14-shot tubular
Barrel: 20"; blued
Stock & Forearm: Checkered hardwood, one-piece semi-pistol grip Monte Carlo stock & forearm; add $10.00 for scope (987T)
Estimated Value: $75.00 - $95.00

Stevens Model No. 57 & 057
Caliber: 22 long rifle
Action: Semi-automatic; repeating
Magazine: 5-shot clip
Barrel: 24"
Stock & Forearm: Plain walnut pistol grip stock & forearm; black tipped forearm on 57; 057 has peep sight
Estimated Value: $85.00 - $110.00

Stevens Model No. 76 & 076
Same as 057 & 57 except: 15-shot tubular magazine
Estimated Value: $90.00 - $120.00

Stevens/Universal

Stevens Model No. 887-T

Steven Model 887-T
Similar to the Model 887 with a 4X scope
Estimated Value: $80.00 - $100.00

Stevens Model 887
Caliber: 22 long rifle
Action: Semi-automatic
Magazine: 15-shot tubular
Barrel: 20"; blued
Stock & Forearm: Checkered hardwood, one-piece semi-pistol grip stock & forearm
Estimated Value: $70.00 - $90.00

Universal

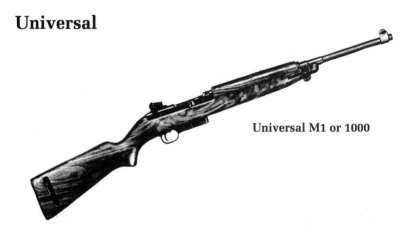

Universal M1 or 1000

Universal M1 or 1000 & 1003
Similar to the U.S. M1 Carbine with a 5-shot detachable clip. Made in 30 caliber since the mid 1960's; add $50.00 for scope & detachable mount; see also Iver Johnson
Estimated Value: $145.00 - $180.00

Universal 1020, 1020 TB,
1020 TCO & 1030
Similar to the 1000 with a Monte Carlo stock & a water resistant teflon finish in green, blue, tan, black, or gray; currently produced as 1020 TB (black) & 1020 TCO (green), 1030 (gray).
Estimated Value: $180.00 - $225.00

Universal 440 Vulcan

Universal M1 or 1000 Deluxe

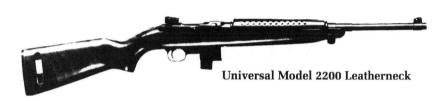

Universal Model 2200 Leatherneck

Universal 440 Vulcan
Caliber: 44 magnum
Action: Slide action; hammerless; repeating
Magazine: 5-shot clip
Barrel: 18¼"; carbine
Stock & Forearm: Walnut semi-pistol grip stock & slide handle
Estimated Value: $170.00 - $215.00

Universal M1 or 1000 Deluxe, 1005 SB, 1010N, 1015G & 1011
Same as the 1000 with a Monte Carlo stock; also available in nickel, gold-plate or chrome
Estimated Value:
   1005SB (Blue): $140.00 - $175.00
   1010N (Nickel): $150.00 - $190.00
   1015G (Gold): $185.00 - $230.00
   1011 (Chrome): $145.00 - $185.00

Universal Ferret
Similar to the M1 except: Monte Carlo stock; no sights; 256 caliber
Estimated Value: $155.00 - $195.00

Universal Model 1035, 1040 & 1045
Similar to the Model 1020 except: military stock
Estimated Value: $165.00 - $210.00

Universal Model 1006
Similar to the Model 1005SB except: stainless steel
Estimated Value: $175.00 - $220.00

Universal Model 2200 Leatherneck
Similar to the Model 1003 except: 22 caliber; produced from the early 1980's to mid 1980's
Estimated Value: $150.00 - $185.00

Weatherby

Weatherby Deluxe

Weatherby Deluxe
Similar to the Magnum Deluxe but in 270 Win. and 30-06 calibers.
Estimated Value: $460.00 - $575.00

Weatherby Magnum Deluxe
Caliber: 378 mag., 300 mag., 375 mag., 7mm mag., 270 mag., 257 mag., or 220 Rocket
Action: Bolt action; Mauser-type
Magazine: 3-shot
Barrel: 24" or 26"; blued
Stock & Forearm: Checkered wood Monte Carlo one-piece pistol grip stock & tapered forearm; recoil pad; swivels; cheekpiece
Estimated Value: $540.00 - $675.00

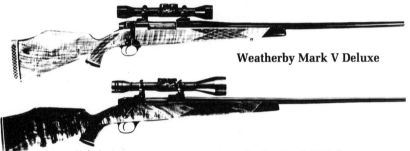

Weatherby Mark V Deluxe

Weatherby Varmintmaster

Weatherby Fibermark
Similar to the Mark V Deluxe except: one-piece black fiberglass stock & forearm; introduced in the mid 1980's
Estimated Value: $825.00 - $1,035.00

Weatherby Varmintmaster
A scaled-down version of the Mark V Deluxe in 22-250 or 224 Weatherby magnum; 24" or 26" barrel; add 5% for Lazermark Series
Estimated Value: $740.00 - $925.00

Weatherby Mark V Deluxe
Caliber: 240, 257, 270, 7mm, 30-06, 300 Weatherby mag., 340 mag., 378 Weatherby mag., or 460 Weatherby mag.
Action: Bolt action; repeating
Magazine: 2, 3, or 4-shot, depending on caliber
Barrel: 24" or 26"; blued
Stock & Forearm: Checkered walnut Monte Carlo one-piece pistol grip stock & tapered forearm; cheekpiece; recoil pad; swivels; available in Euromark & Lazermark series with custom extras; add 5% for Euromark & 12% for Lazermark; add 3% for 340 magnum caliber, 18% for 378 Win. caliber, & 32% for 460 magnum caliber
Estimated Value: $735.00 - $920.00

Weatherby Alaskan

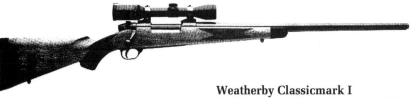

Weatherby Weathermark

Weatherby Classicmark I

Weatherby Weathermark
Caliber: 240 Wby. mag., 257 Wby. mag., 270 Wby. mag., 270 Win., 7mm Rem. mag., 7mm Wby. mag., 30-06, 300 Wby. mag., or 340 Wby. mag.
Action: Bolt action; repeating
Magazine: 4-shot (3-shot magnum) box; with hinged floor plate
Barrel: 22", 24", or 26"; blued
Stock & Forearm: Checkered synthetic composite one-piece stock and forearm, pistol grip; recoil pad, swivels
Estimated Value: $600.00 - $ 750.00

Weatherby Alaskan
Similar to the Weathermark except: non-glare stainless electroless nickel plate finish
Estimated Value: $710.00 - $885.00

Weatherby Classicmark I
Caliber: 240 Wby. mag., 257 Wby. mag., 270 Wby. mag., 270 Win., 7mm Rem. mag., 7mm Wby. mag., 30-06, 300 Wby. mag., 340 Wby. mag., 375 H&H mag., 378 Wby. mag., 416 Wby. mag., or 460 Wby. mag.
Action: Bolt action; repeating
Magazine: 4-shot (3-shot magnum) box; with hinged floor plate
Barrel: 22", 24", or 26"; blued
Stock & Forearm: Oil-finished, checkered walnut, Monte Carlo pistol grip, one-piece stock & forearm; recoil pad, swivels; add 15-20% for magnum calibers
Estimated Value: $700.00 - $880.00

Weatherby Classicmark II
Similar to the Classicmark I except: deluxe American Walnut stock and forearm with satin-finish metalwork; add 15-20% for magnum calibers
Estimated Value: 1,065.00 - $1,330.00

Weatherby

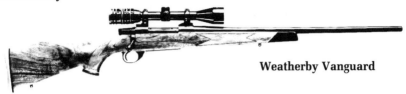

Weatherby Vanguard

Weatherby Vanguard VGL

Weatherby Vanguard VGX

Weatherby Weatherguard
Caliber: 223 Rem., 243 Rem., 270 Win., 7mm-08 Rem., 7mm Rem. magnum, 30-06, or 308 Win.
Action: Bolt action; repeating
Magazine: 4-shot (3-shot magnum) box; with hinged floor plate
Barrel: 24"; blued
Stock & Forearm: Checkered synthetic composite one-piece pistol grip stock and forearm; recoil pad; swivels
Estimated Value: $300.00 - $370.00

Weatherby Vanguard VGX, VGS, VGL
Caliber: 22-250, 25-06, 243, 264, 270, 30-06, 7mm Rem. mag., or 300 Win. mag.
Action: Bolt action; repeating
Magazine: 5-shot (3-shot magnum) box, with hinged floor plate
Barrel: 24"; blued
Stock & Forearm: Checkered walnut; Monte Carlo pistol grip; one-piece stock & forearm; recoil pad; swivels; VGX has deluxe finish
Estimated Value: $340.00 - $425.00

Weatherby Classic II
Similar to the Vanguard with satin finish; checkered stock and forearm
Estimated Value: $450.00 - $560.00

Weatherby Mark XXII (Clip)

Weatherby Mark XXII Deluxe
Caliber: 22 long rifle
Action: Semi-automatic; hammerless
Magazine: 5 or 10-shot clip; 15-shot tubular
Barrel: 24"; blued
Stock & Forearm: Checkered walnut Monte Carlo one-piece pistol grip stock & tapered forearm; swivels
Estimated Value: $270.00 - $340.00

Weatherby Vanguard Fiberguard
Caliber: 223, 243, 270, 7mm Rem. magnum, 30-06, or 308 Win.
Action: Bolt action; repeating; short action
Magazine: 6-shot in 223; 5-shot in 243, 270, 30-06 & 308; 3-shot in 7mm Rem. magnum
Barrel: 20"; blued
Stock & Forearm: All-weather fiberglass one-piece semi-pistol grip stock & forearm; forest green wrinkle finish with black butt pad
Estimated Value: $400.00 - $500.00

Western Field

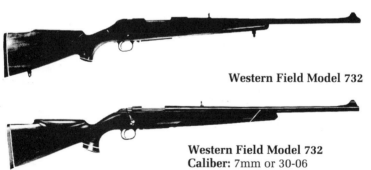

Western Field Model 732

Western Field Model 730

Western Field Model 730
Similar to 732; produced until mid 1970's.
Estimated Value: $160.00 - $200.00

Western Field Model 732
Caliber: 7mm or 30-06
Action: Bolt action; repeating; hammerless
Magazine: 4 or 5-shot tubular (depending on caliber)
Barrel: 22"; blued
Stock & Forearm: Checkered walnut Monte Carlo one-piece pistol grip stock & forearm; swivels
Estimated Value: $175.00 - $220.00

Western Field

Western Field Model 780

Western Field Model 775

Western Field Bolt Action Repeater

Western Field Bolt Action Repeater
Caliber: 22 short, long, long rifle or 22 WMR
Action: Bolt action; repeating
Magazine: 7-shot clip in 22; 5-shot in 22 WMR
Barrel: 24"; blued
Stock & Forearm: Walnut one-piece pistol grip stock & forearm
Estimated Value: $60.00 - $75.00

Western Field Model 780
Caliber: 243 or 308
Action: Bolt action; repeating
Magazine: 5-shot tubular
Barrel: 22"; blued
Stock & Forearm: Checkered walnut Monte Carlo one-piece pistol grip stock & forearm
Estimated Value: $160.00 - $200.00

Western Field Model 775 & 776
Similar to the 780; produced until mid 1970's.
Estimated Value: $145.00 - $180.00

Western Field Model 842

Western Field Bolt Action
Caliber: 30-06
Action: Bolt action; repeating
Magazine: 4-shot, hinged floorplate
Barrel: 22"; blued; round
Stock & Forearm: Smooth hardwood one-piece pistol grip stock & forearm with sling swivels
Estimated Value: $155.00 - $190.00

Western Field Model 842
Caliber: 22 short, long, or long rifle
Action: Bolt action; repeating
Magazine: Tubular; 18 long rifle, 20 longs, 22 shorts
Barrel: 24"; blued
Stock & Forearm: Walnut Monte Carlo one-piece pistol grip stock & forearm
Estimated Value: $65.00 - $80.00

Western Field 72

Western Field Model 78 Deluxe
Caliber: 7mm mag. or 30-06
Action: Bolt action
Magazine: 3-shot rotary magazine in 7mm, 4-shot in 30-06
Barrel: 24" in 7mm; 22" in 30-06
Stock & Forearm: Checkered walnut pistol grip stock & forearm; swivels
Estimated Value: $160.00 - $200.00

Western Field Model 72
Caliber: 30-30
Action: Lever-action; exposed hammer; repeating; side ejection
Magazine: 6-shot tubular
Barrel: 18" or 20"; blued
Stock & Forearm: Walnut two-piece pistol grip stock & forearm; barrel band; fluted comb
Estimated Value: $135.00 - $165.00

Western Field Model 740
Similar to Model 72 except: recoil pad; 20" barrel
Estimated Value: $140.00 - $170.00

Western Field Model 815
Caliber: 22 short, long, or long rifle
Action: Bolt action; single-shot; hammerless
Magazine: None; single-shot
Barrel: 24"; blued
Stock & Forearm: Wood Monte Carlo one-piece pistol grip stock & forearm
Estimated Value: $45.00 - $60.00

Western Field Model 79
Caliber: 30-30
Action: Lever-action; exposed hammer; repeating; side ejection
Magazine: 6-shot tubular, side load
Barrel: 20"; blued; round
Stock & Forearm: Smooth hardwood pistol grip stock & forearm
Estimated Value: $125.00 - $160.00

Western Field Model 865
Caliber: 22 short, long, or long rifle
Action: Lever-action; hammerless; repeating
Magazine: Tubular; 13 long rifle, 15 longs, or 20 shorts
Barrel: 20"; blued
Stock & Forearm: Wood Monte Carlo pistol grip stock & forearm; barrel band; swivels
Estimated Value: $80.00 - $100.00

Western Field Model 895

Western Field Model 895
Caliber: 22 long rifle
Action: Semi-automatic; hammerless
Magazine: 18-shot tubular
Barrel: 24"; blued
Stock & Forearm: Checkered walnut Monte Carlo pistol grip stock & forearm
Estimated Value: $70.00 - $85.00

Western Field/Winchester

Western Field Model 846

Western Field Semi-Automatic 895 Carbine
Caliber: 22 long rifle
Action: Semi-automatic; hammerless
Magazine: 15-shot tubular
Barrel: 21"
Stock & Forearm: Smooth hardwood one-piece pistol grip stock & forearm
Estimated Value: $70.00 - $85.00

Western Field Model 850
Caliber: 22 long rifle
Action: Semi-automatic; hammerless
Magazine: 7-shot clip
Barrel: 18"; blued
Stock & Forearm: Wood one-piece semi-pistol grip stock & tapered forearm
Estimated Value: $65.00 - $80.00

Western Field Model 846
Caliber: 22 long rifle
Action: Semi-automatic; hammerless
Magazine: 15-shot tubular, in stock
Barrel: 18½"; blued
Stock & Forearm: Checkered wood one-piece pistol grip stock & forearm; barrel band; swivels
Estimated Value: $75.00 - $90.00

Winchester

Winchester Model 1900

Winchester Model 02
Similar to the Model 1900 except: extended trigger guard; addition of 22 long rifle caliber; made from about 1902 to the early 1930's
Estimated Value: $180.00 - $225.00

Winchester Model 1900
Caliber: 22 short or long
Action: Bolt action; single shot; pull cocking piece
Magazine: None; single-shot
Barrel: 18"; blued; round
Stock & Forearm: Plain one-piece straight grip stock & forearm; made from 1900 to 1903
Estimated Value: $160.00 - $200.00

Winchester Thumb Trigger

**Winchester Thumb Trigger
(Model 02)**
Similar to the Model 02 except: no trigger; the gun is discharged by pushing a button located behind the cocking piece; made until the early 1920's
Estimated Value: $240.00 - $300.00

Winchester Model 04
Similar to the Model 02 except: 21" barrel & lipped forearm; made from 1904 to the early 1930's
Estimated Value: $150.00 - $190.00

Winchester Model 59

Winchester Model 60

Winchester Model 60A

Winchester Model 58
Similar to the Model 1900 single shot; made from the late 1920's to early 1930's
Estimated Value: $130.00 - $160.00

Winchester Model 60
Similar to the Model 59 except: 23" or 27" barrel; made from the early to mid 1930's
Estimated Value: $140.00 - $175.00

Winchester Model 59
Similar to the Model 58 except: 23" barrel; made from about 1930 to 1931
Estimated Value: $135.00 - $165.00

Winchester Model 60A
Similar to the Model 60 except: special Lyman sights; swivels; made to about 1940
Estimated Value: $130.00 - $170.00

Winchester

Winchester Model 67

Winchester Model 68

Winchester Model 55

Winchester Model 68
Similar to the Model 67 except: peep rear sight
Estimated Value: $90.00 - $115.00

Winchester Model 67
Caliber: 22 short, long, or long rifle
Action: Bolt action; single shot
Magazine: None; single-shot
Barrel: 27"; blued
Stock & Forearm: Plain walnut one-piece semi-pistol grip stock & fluted forearm
Estimated Value: $80.00 - $100.00

Winchester Model 67 Boy's
Similar to the Model 67 except: 20" barrel & youth stock
Estimated Value: $70.00 - $90.00

Winchester Model 677
Similar to the Model 67 with no sights; made only in the late 1930's
Estimated Value: $75.00 - $100.00

Winchester Model 55
Caliber: 22 short, long, or long rifle
Action: Single-shot
Magazine: None
Barrel: 22"
Stock & Forearm: Plain wood one-piece semi-pistol grip stock & forearm
Estimated Value: $75.00 - $90.00

Winchester Lee

Winchester Lee Musket
Similar to the Winchester Lee except: military sights; full-length musket forearm; 28" barrel; swivels
Estimated Value: $550.00 - $700.00

Winchester Lee
Caliber: 6mm (236)
Action: Bolt action; repeating
Magazine: 5-shot detachable box
Barrel: 24"; round; nickel steel
Stock & Forearm: One-piece semi-pistol grip stock & fluted, lipped forearm; made from the late 1890's to early 1900's
Estimated Value: $650.00 - $800.00

Winchester Model 57

Winchester Model 56

Winchester Model 57
Similar to the Model 56 except: longer, unlipped forearm; barrel band; swivels; special Lyman sights; target model
Estimated Value: $240.00 - $300.00

Winchester Model 56
Caliber: 22 short or long rifle only
Action: Bolt action; repeating
Magazine: 5 or 20-shot detachable box
Barrel: 22"; blued
Stock & Forearm: Plain walnut one-piece semi-pistol grip stock & lipped forearm
Estimated Value: $200.00 - $250.00

Winchester Model 52

Winchester Model 52 Sporting

Winchester Model 52-B

Winchester Model 52
Caliber: 22 long rifle
Action: Bolt action; repeating
Magazine: 5-shot box
Barrel: 28"; blued
Stock & Forearm: Plain walnut one-piece pistol grip stock & forearm
Estimated Value: $360.00 - $450.00

Winchester Model 52 Heavy Barrel
Similar to the Model 52 except: heavier barrel & special Lyman sights
Estimated Value: $380.00 - $475.00

Winchester Model 52 Sporting
Similar to the Model 52 except: 24" barrel; special Lyman sights; checkering; cheekpiece
Estimated Value: $380.00 - $475.00

Winchester Model 52-B
Similar to the Model 52 except: improved action; regular or high comb stock
Estimated Value: $540.00 - $675.00

Winchester Model 52-B
Heavy Barrel
Similar to the Model 52-B except: heavy barrel
Estimated Value: $400.00 - $500.00

Winchester

Winchester Model 52-B Bull Gun

Winchester Model 52-B Sporting

Winchester Model 52-C Bull Gun

Winchester Model 52-C

Winchester Model 52-D Target

Winchester Model 52-B Bull Gun
Similar to the Model 52-B Heavy
Barrel except: still heavier barrel
Estimated Value: $400.00 - $510.00

Winchester Model 52-B Sporting
Similar to the Model 52 Sporting
with a 52-B action
Estimated Value: $380.00 - $475.00

Winchester Model 52-C
Similar to the 52-B with more
improvements on the action; high
comb stock
Estimated Value: $560.00 - $695.00

**Winchester Model 52-C
Heavy Barrel**
Similar to the Model 52 Heavy
Barrel with a 52-C action
Estimated Value: $400.00 - $500.00

Winchester Model 52-C Bull Gun
Similar to the Model 52-B Bull Gun
with a 52-C action
Estimated Value: $440.00 - $550.00

Winchester Model 52-D Target
Similar to the 52-C except: single
shot; hand stop on forearm
Estimated Value: $420.00 - $525.00

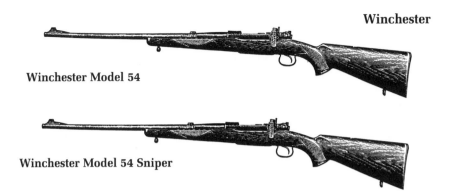

Winchester Model 54

Winchester Model 54 Sniper

Winchester Model 54
Caliber: 270, 7x57, 30-30, 30-06, 7.65x53mm, 9x57mm, 7mm, 250-3000, 22 Hornet, 220 Swift, or 257 Roberts
Action: Bolt action; repeating
Magazine: 5-shot box; non-detachable
Barrel: 24"; blued
Stock & Forearm: Checkered walnut one-piece pistol grip stock & forearm
Estimated Value: $390.00 - $520.00

Winchester Model 54 Carbine
Similar to the Model 54 except: 20" barrel; no checkering
Estimated Value: $395.00 - $525.00

Winchester Model 54 Sporting (Improved)
Similar to the Model 54 except: improved action; 26" barrel; additional calibers
Estimated Value: $450.00 - $560.00

Winchester Model 54 Carbine (Improved)
Similar to the Model 54 Carbine with improved action
Estimated Value: $480.00 - $600.00

Winchester Model 54 Super
Similar to the Model 54 except: cheekpiece; select wood; deluxe finish; swivels
Estimated Value: $600.00 - $750.00

Winchester Model 54 Sniper
Similar to the Model 54 except: 26" heavy barrel; special Lyman sights; 30-06 caliber only
Estimated Value: $465.00 - $620.00

Winchester Model 54 Sniper Match
Deluxe version of the Model 54 Sniper with high-quality finish
Estimated Value: $550.00 - $685.00

Winchester Model 54 National Match
Similar to the Model 54 with special Lyman sights & marksman stock
Estimated Value: $500.00 - $620.00

Winchester Model 54 Target
Similar to the Model 54 with 24" barrel & special Lyman sights
Estimated Value: $520.00 - $650.00

Winchester Model 69

Winchester Model 69 Target
Similar to the Model 69 except: peep sights & swivels
Estimated Value: $115.00 - $145.00

Winchester Model 69
Caliber: 22 short, long, or long rifle
Action: Bolt action; repeating
Magazine: 5 or 10-shot detachable box
Barrel: 25"; blued
SStock & Forearm: Plain walnut one-piece semi-pistol grip stock & forearm
Estimated Value: $100.00 - $130.00

Winchester Model 69 Match
Similar to the Model 69 Target except: special Lyman sights
Estimated Value: $130.00 - $160.00

Winchester Model 697
Similar to the Model 69 except: no sights
Estimated Value: $120.00 - $150.00

Winchester Model 70 (1937)

Winchester Model 70 XTR

Winchester Model 70 (1937)
Caliber: 375 H&H mag., 300 H&H mag., 308 Win., 30-06, 7x57mm, 270 Win., 257 Roberts, 250-3000, 243, 220, or 22 Hornet
Action: Bolt action; repeating
Magazine: 5-shot box; 4-shot box in magnum
Barrel: 24" or 26"; blued
Stock & Forearm: Checkered walnut one-piece pistol grip stock & forearm; made from about 1937 to 1963; add $150.00 for mint, unfired condition
Estimated Value: $650.00 - $800.00

Winchester Model 70 (1964)
Similar to the Model 70 (1937) except: improvements: Monte Carlo stock; swivels; made from about 1964 until 1970; in calibers 22-250, 22 Rem., 225, 243, 270, 308, or 30-06
Estimated Value: $275.00 - $360.00

Winchester Model 70 (1971), 70 XTR (1978), 70 XTR Sporter (1983)
Similar to the Model 70 (1964) with improvements; made from 1971 to present; calibers 270 Win., 30-06, 25-06 (1985), 308 Win. (1987), or 243 (1988)
Estimated Value: $280.00 - $350.00

Winchester Model 70 Target (1937)

Winchester Model 70A & 70A XTR
Similar to the Model 70 (1971) except: special steel barrel; adjustable sights; made from the early 1970's to about 1981; 4-shot or 3-shot (magnum) box magazine; add $20.00 for 264 Win. mag., 7mm Rem. mag., or 300 Win. mag.
Estimated Value: $225.00 - $300.00

Winchester Model 70 XTR Featherwieght
Similar to the Model 70 XTR except: calibers 22-250, 223, 243, 308, 270 Win., 257 Roberts, 7mm Mauser, or 30-06 recoil pad; lipped forearm; decorative checkering; 22" barrel
Estimated Value: $280.00 - $350.00

Winchester Model 70 XTR European Featherweight
Similar to the Model 70XTR Featherweight except: caliber 6.55x55 Swedish Mauser; produced in 1986 & 1987
Estimated Value: $275.00 - $365.00

Winchester Model 70 Lightweight Carbine
Similar to the Model 70XTR Featherweight with different outward appearance, 20" barrel; in calibers 270 Win., 30-06 Springfield, 22-250 Rem., 223 Rem., 243 Win., 308 Win., or 250 Savage; produced 1986 & 1987
Estimated Value: $240.00 - $320.00

Winchester Model 70 Super (1937)
Similar to the Model 70 (1937) except: swivels; deluxe finish; cheekpiece; made to early 1960's
Estimated Value: $850.00 - $1,000.00

Winchester Model 70 Super
Similar to the Model 70 Super (1937) with recoil pad; select wood; made from mid 1960's to mid 1970's
Estimated Value: $280.00 - $350.00

Winchester Model 70 Target (1937)
Similar to the Model 70 (1937) except: 24" barrel & improved stock; made until about 1963
Estimated Value: $675.00 - $900.00

Winchester Model 70 Target (1964) & 1971
Similar to the Model 70 Target (1937) except: aluminum hand stop; Model (1971) has minor improvements; calibers 30-06, 308 Win., or 308 Int'l Army; add $130.00 for Int'l Army
Estimated Value: $320.00 - $400.00

Winchester Model 70 African (1971)

Winchester Model 70 National Match
Similar to the Model 70 (1937) except: marksman stock in 30-06 caliber; made to the early 1960's
Estimated Value: $640.00 - $800.00

Winchester Model 70 Mannlicher
Similar to the Model 70 (1964) except: full-length forearm; 19" barrel; calibers 243, 270, 308, or 30-06; made to the early 1970's
Estimated Value: $300.00 - $375.00

Winchester Model 70 Varmint (1956), (1964) (1971), & 70 XTR Varmint
Similar to the Model 70 (1937) except: heavy 24" or 26" barrel; improvements made along with other Model 70's; calibers 222 Rem., 22-250, or 243 Win.; add 90% for pre-1964 models; discontinued 1988.
Estimated Value: $270.00 - $360.00

Winchester Model 70 Featherweight Sporter
A lightweight rifle similar to the Model 70 (1937) with improved stock; made from the early 1950's to 1960's
Estimated Value: $660.00 - $825.00

Winchester Model 70 Featherweight Super
Similar to the Model 70 Featherweight Sporter except deluxe finish; cheekpiece; swivels; made after 1964
Estimated Value: $240.00 - $325.00

Winchester Model 70 African (1971)
Similar to the Model 70 African (1964) with floating barrel; caliber 458 Win. mag; discontinued about 1981
Estimated Value: $420.00 - $525.00

Winchester Model 70 African (1964)
Similar to the Model 70 African (1956) with improvements; made to 1970
Estimated Value: $340.00 - $425.00

Winchester Model 70 African (1956)
Similar to the Model 70 (1937) Super Grade with recoil pad; Monte Carlo stock; 3-shot magazine; 24" barrel; 458 caliber only; made to 1963
Estimated Value: $960.00 - $1,200.00

Winchester Model 70 Alaskan
Similar to the Model 70 (1937) except: 24" or 26" barrel; made in the early 1960's
Estimated Value: $800.00 - $1,000.00

Winchester Model 70 Magnum

Winchester Model 70 Deluxe

Winchester Model 70 Westerner
Similar to the Model 70 Alaskan (1956); made in the early 1960's
Estimated Value: $640.00 - $800.00

Winchester Model 70 Westerner (1982)
Similar to the Model 70XTR (1978) except: 22" barrel; 4-shot magazine in calibers 243 Win., 270 Win., 308 win., or 30-06 Springfield; 24" barrel & 3-shot magazine in calibers 7mm Rem. mag. or 300 Win. mag.; introduced in 1982; discontinued in 1984
Estimated Value: $320.00 - $400.00

Winchester Model 70 Winlite
Caliber: 270, 30-06, 7mm Rem. mag., 300 Win. mag., 300 Weatherby mag., or 338 Win. mag.
Action: Bolt action; repeating
Magazine: 4-shot in 270 or 30-06; 3-shot in magnum calibers
Barrel: 22" in 270 & 30-06; 24" in magnum calibers
Stock & Forearm: Fiberglass reinforced one-piece stock & forearm with thermoplastic bedding for receiver & barrel; made from 1986 to 1991
Estimated Value: $380.00 - $475.00

Winchester Model 70 Deluxe (1964)
Similar to the Model 70 (1964) except: Monte Carlo stock; recoil pad; deluxe features; made to the early 1970's
Estimated Value: $320.00 - $400.00

Winchester Model 70 Magnum (1964)
Similar to the Model 70 (1964) except: Monte Carlo stock; recoil pad; swivels; 3-shot magazine; made to the early 1970's
Estimated Value: $335.00 - $400.00

Winchester Model 70XTR & 70 Sporter Mag.
Caliber: 22-250, 223, 243, 25-06 Rem., 264 Win. mag., 270 Win., 300 Win mag., 338 Win. mag.; 7mm Rem. mag., or 300 Weatherby mag.
Action: Bolt action; repeating
Magazine: 3-shot box
Barrel: 24"; blued
Stock & Forearm: Checkered walnut Monte Carlo one-piece pistol grip stock & forearm; cheekpiece; recoil pad; swivels; introduced in 1982
Estimated Value: $325.00 - $405.00

Winchester Model 70XTR & 70 Super Express Mag.
Similar to the Model 70 XTR Sporter Magnum except: 22" barrel in 458 Win. magnum caliber; 24" barrel in 375 H & H magnum caliber; introduced in 1982
Estimated Value: $490.00 - $610.00

Winchester

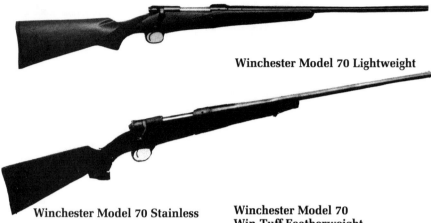

Winchester Model 70 Lightweight

Winchester Model 70 Stainless

Winchester Model 70 Win-Cam Featherweight
Similar to the Model 70 Featherweight Super except: laminated green & brown camouflage stock; calibers 270 Win. & 30-06; discontinued in 1991
Estimated Value: $285.00 - $355.00

Winchester Model 70 Lightweight
Similar to the Model 70XTR except: 22" barrel; calibers: 22-250 Rem., 223 Rem., 243 Win., 270 Win., 280 Win., 30-06 spring., or 308 Win.; swivels
Estimated Value: $280.00 - $350.00

Winchester Model 70 Win-Tuff Lightweight
Similar to the Model 70 Lightweight except: laminated stock of dye-shaded hardwoods; in calibers: 223 Rem., 243 Win., 270 Win., 308 Win., or 30-06; short or long action
Estimated Value: $280.00 - $350.00

Winchester Model 70 Win-Tuff Featherweight
Similar to the Model 70 Featherweight Super except: laminated stock of dye-shaded hardwood; available in calibers: 243 Win., 270 Win., or 30-06 Spring; discontinued in 1991
Estimated Value: $285.00 - $355.00

Winchester Model 70 Stainless
Caliber: 270, 30-06, 7mm Rem. magnum, 300 Win. mag., or 338 Win. mag.
Action: Bolt action; repeating; 3-position safety
Magazine: 5-shot in 270 & 30-06; 3-shot in mag. calibers; hinged floorplate
Barrel: Blued; 22" in 270 and 30-06; 24" in magnum calibers
Stock & Forearm: Black synthetic composite impregnated with fiberglass and graphite one-piece checkered stock and forearm; rubber recoil pad; introduced in 1992
Estimated Value: $345.00 - $430.00

Winchester Model 70 SSM
Same as the Model 70 Stainless except: 24" barrel for all calibers; black matte finish steel barrel and receiver; introduced in 1992
Estimated Value: $330.00 - $415.00

Winchester Model 70 Super Grade

Winchester Model 70 Varmint

Winchester Model 70 Varmint
Caliber: 22-250, 223, 243, or 308
Action: Bolt action; repeating; 3-position safety
Magazine: 5-shot; hinged floorplate
Barrel: 26"; counter-bored heavy barrel, blued or matte finish
Stock & Forearm: Checkered walnut one-piece stock and forearm with cheekpiece; or black composite checkered matte finish stock and forearm (in 1992) in 308 caliber; introduced in the late 1980's
Estimated Value: $335.00 - $420.00

Winchester Model 70 Super Grade
Caliber: 270 , 30-06 , 7mm Rem. mag., 300 Win. mag., or 338 Win. mag.
Action: Bolt action; repeating; 3-position safety
Magazine: 5-shot in 270 or 30-06; 3-shot in magnum calibers; hinged floorplate
Barrel: 24"; blued
Stock & Forearm: Select walnut, one-piece checkered sculptured cheekpiece stock and forearm with satin finish; introduced in the late 1980's
Estimated Value: $600.00 - $745.00

Winchester Model 70 Sporter Win-Tuff

Winchester Model 70 Sporter DBM
Caliber: 270, 30-06, 7mm Rem. magnum, or 300 Win. mag.
Action: Bolt action; repeating
Magazine: 3-shot detachable box
Barrel: 24"; steel; blued
Stock & Forearm: Checkered walnut one-piece stock and forearm with cheekpiece; introduced in 1992
Estimated Value: $340.00 - $425.00

Winchester Model 70 Sporter Win-Tuff
Caliber: 270, 30-06, 7mm Rem. magnum, 300 Win. mag., 300 Wby. mag., or 338 Win. mag.
Action: Bolt action; repeating; 3-position safety
Magazine: 5-shot in 270 and 30-06; 3-shot in magnum calibers; hinged floorplate
Barrel: 24"; blued
Stock & Forearm: Brown laminated checkered, one-piece stock and forearm with cheekpiece; introduced in 1992
Estimated Value: $325.00 - $405.00

Winchester

Winchester Model 70 Featherweight Classic

Winchester Model 70 Featherweight Classic

Same as the Model 70 Featherweight Win-Tuff except: calibers 270, 280, and 30-06; checkered walnut stock and forearm; introduced in 1992
Estimated Value: $450.00 - $560.00

Winchester Model 70 Featherweight Win-Tuff

Caliber: 22-250, 223 Rem., 243 Win., 308 Win., or 30-06
Action: Bolt action; repeating; 3-position safety
Magazine: 5-shot; hinged floorplate; 6-shot in 243 Rem.
Barrel: 22"; blued
Stock & Forearm: Laminated brown hardwood one-piece checkered stock and forearm with a schnabel fore end (lipped); previously made in the 1980's in 243, 270, and 30-06 calibers; reintroduced in 1992 with larger selection of calibers
Estimated Value: $325.00 - $405.00

Winchester Model 72

Winchester Model 75 Target

Winchester Model 75 Sporter

Winchester Model 72

Caliber: 22 short, long, or long rifle
Action: Bolt action; repeating
Magazine: Tubular; 15 long rifle, 16 longs, or 20 shorts
Barrel: 25"; blued
Stock & Forearm: Plain walnut one-piece semi-pistol grip stock & forearm
Estimated Value: $115.00 - $145.00

Winchester Model 75 Target

Caliber: 22 long rifle
Action: Bolt action; repeating
Magazine: 5 or 10-shot detachable box
Barrel: 28"; blued
Stock & Forearm: Plain walnut one-piece pistol grip stock & forearm
Estimated Value: $230.00 - $290.00

Winchester Model 75 Sporter

Similar to the Model 75 Target except: checkering; 24" barrel
Estimated Value: $240.00 - $300.00

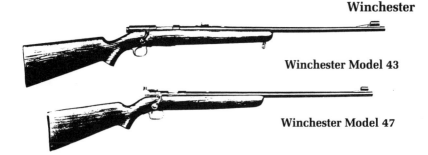

Winchester Model 43

Winchester Model 47

Winchester Model 43
Caliber: 218 Bee, 22 Hornet, 25-20, or 32-30 (25-20 & 32-30 dropped in 1950)
Action: Bolt action; repeating
Magazine: 3-shot detachable
Barrel: 24"; blued
Stock & Forearm: Plain wood one-piece semi-pistol grip stock & forearm; swivels
Estimated Value: $290.00 - $360.00

Winchester Model 43 Special
Similar to the Model 43 except: checkering
Estimated Value: $310.00 - $390.00

Winchester Model 47
Similar to the Model 43 except: 22 short, long, or long rifle; single-shot; 25" barrel; made from the late 1940's to mid 1950's
Estimated Value: $85.00 - $110.00

Winchester Model 670

Winchester Model 770

Winchester Model 670
Caliber: 243, 270, 30-06, 225, 243, 270, 308, 30-06 , 264 Win. mag., or 300 Win. mag.
Action: Bolt action; repeating
Magazine: 4-shot box; 3-shot box in magnum
Barrel: 19", 22", or 24"; blued
Stock & Forearm: Checkered hardwood Monte Carlo one-piece pistol grip stock & forearm
Estimated Value: $220.00 - $270.00

Winchester Model 770
Caliber: 22-250, 222, 243, 270, 30-06
Action: Bolt action; repeating
Magazine: 4-shot box
Barrel: 22"; blued
Stock & Forearm: Checkered walnut Monte Carlo one-piece pistol grip stock & forearm; swivels
Estimated Value: $230.00 - $290.00

Winchester Model 770 Magnum
Similar to the Model 770 except: magnum calibers with recoil pad & 24" barrel; 3-shot magazine
Estimated Value: $250.00 - $310.00

Winchester

Winchester Model 310
Caliber: 22 short, long, or long rifle
Action: Bolt action; single shot
Magazine: None; single- shot
Barrel: 22"; blued
Stock & Forearm: Checkered walnut Monte Carlo one-pistol grip stock & forearm; swivels
Estimated Value: $60.00 - $75.00

Winchester Model 320
Similar to the Model 310 except: bolt action repeating; 5-shot clip
Estimated Value: $85.00 - $110.00

Winchester Model 121

Winchester Model 121
Caliber: 22 short, long, or long rifle
Action: Bolt action; single-shot
Magazine: None; single-shot
Barrel: 20½"; blued
Stock & Forearm: Plain one-piece semi-pistol grip stock & forearm
Estimated Value: $55.00 - $70.00

Winchester Model 121 Youth
Similar to the Model 121 except: shorter barrel & youth stock
Estimated Value: $60.00 - $75.00

Winchester Model 121 Deluxe
Similar to the Model 121 except: Monte Carlo stock; swivels
Estimated Value: $60.00 - $80.00

Winchester Model 131
Similar to the Model 121 except: semi-Monte Carlo stock; 7-shot clip magazine; bolt action repeater
Estimated Value: $65.00 - $85.00

Winchester Model 141
Similar to the 131 except: tubular magazine
Estimated Value: $75.00 - $90.00

Winchester Ranger Youth/Ladies & 70 Ranger Youth/Ladies
A scaled down bolt action (short action) carbine for young or small shooters; caliber 243 Win., or 308 Win.; 20" barrel; plain wood, one-piece stock & forearm; swivels
Estimated Value: $265.00 - $330.00

Winchester Ranger & Model 70 Ranger
Caliber: 223, 243, 270 Win., or 30-06
Action: Bolt action; repeating
Magazine: 4-shot
Barrel: 22"; blued
Stock & Forearm: Plain one-piece semi-pistol grip wood stock & forearm
Estimated Value: $255.00 - $320.00

Pocket Guide to Rifles

Winchester Model 92

Winchester Model 1886 Carbine

Winchester Model 1873 Carbine
Similar to the Model 1873 except:
20" barrel; 12-shot magazine; three
models made from 1873 to 1920
Estimated Value: $1,150.00 - $2,700.00

Winchester Model 1873
Caliber: 32-20, 38-40, or 44-40
Action: Lever action; exposed
hammer; repeating
Magazine: 6 or 15-shot tubular
Barrel: 24" or 26"; round, octagon, or
half-octagon
Stock & Forearm: Straight grip stock
& forearm; thousands of this model
were sold by Winchester until 1920;
add $200.00 to $500.00 for Deluxe
engraved models; price range is for
the different models i.e., 1st, 2nd,
and 3rd models
Estimated Value: $1,200.00 - $2,800.00

Winchester Model 1873 Musket
Similar to the Model 1873 except:
30" round barrel, full-length forearm;
17-shot magazine; three models
made from 1873 to 1920
Estimated Value: $1,400.00 - $3,000.00

Winchester Model 92
Caliber: 25-20, 32-30, 38-40, 44-40
Action: Lever action; exposed
hammer; repeating
Magazine: 7 or 13-shot tubular
Barrel: 24"; round, octagon, or half-
octagon
Stock & Forearm: Plain walnut
straight grip stock & forearm; made
from about 1892 to early 1930's
Estimated Value: $680.00 - $850.00

Winchester Model 92 Carbine
Similar to the Model 92 except: 20"
barrel; barrel band; & 5 or 11-shot
magazine; discontinued in the early
1940's
Estimated Value: $720.00 - $900.00

Winchester Model 1886
Caliber: 45-70 or 33 Win.; also other
calibers for early models
Action: Lever action; exposed
hammer; repeating
Magazine: 4 or 8-shot tubular
Barrel: 26"; round, octagon, or half-
octagon
Stock & Forearm: Plain wood
straight grip stock & forearm; made
from the mid 1880's to the mid
1930's
Estimated Value: $620.00 - $1,500.00

Winchester Model 1886 Carbine
Similar to the Model 1886 except:
22" barrel
Estimated Value: $640.00 - $2,000.00

Winchester

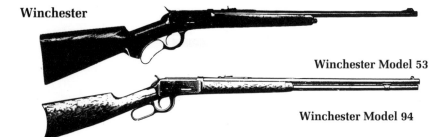

Winchester Model 53

Winchester Model 94

Winchester Model 53
Similar to the Model 92 except: 6 or 7-shot magazine; 22" nickel steel barrel; choice of straight or pistol grip stock; made from the mid 1920's to the early 1930's
Estimated Value: $660.00 - $825.00

Winchester Model 65
Similar to the Model 53 except: 25-20 & 32-30 caliber; semi-pistol grip stock; other minor improvements; made from the early 1930's to late 1940's
Estimated Value: $640.00 - $800.00

Winchester Model 65 (218 Bee)
Similar to the Model 65 except: peep sights; 24" barrel; 218 bee caliber; made from the late 1930's to late 1940's
Estimated Value: $800.00 - $1,000.00

Winchester Model 94
Caliber: 25-35, 30-30, 32 Special, 32-40, or 38-55
Action: Lever action; exposed hammer; repeating
Magazine: 4 or 7-shot tubular
Barrel: 22"or 26"; round, octagon, or half-octagon
Stock & Forearm: Straight stock & forearm; saddle ring on some models; made from 1894 to the late 1930's
Estimated Value: $380.00 - $475.00

Winchester Model 94 Carbine
Similar to the Model 94 except: 20" barrel; barrel band; saddle ring optional; 6-shot magazine; add $200.00 for pre-World War II models; add $400.00 for pre-1925 Models with saddle ring; made to mid 1960's
Estimated Value: $225.00 - $275.00

Winchester Model 94 Standard
Caliber: 30-30, 444 Marlin, 44 magnum, or 45 Colt
Action: Lever action, exposed hammer; repeating; Angle-eject feature added in 1984, listed as "Side eject" in 1986
Magazine: 6-shot
Barrel: 20"; round with barrel band
Stock & Forearm: Plain or checkered wood straight grip stock & forearm; barrel band; made from the mid 1960's to present
Estimated Value: $195.00 - $245.00

Winchester Model 94 Antique
Similar to the Model 94 Standard except: case hardened, scroll design frame; 30-30 caliber; made from the late 1960's to 1984
Estimated Value: $180.00 - $225.00

Winchester Model 94 Trapper
Same as the Model 94 Standard except: 16" barrel; calibers 44 Rem. magnum, 44 S&W Special, 45 Colt, or 357; Magazine capacity is 5-shot in 30-30 & 9-shot in 357, 44, or 45
Estimated Value: $195.00 - $245.00

Winchester Model 94XTR

Winchester Model 94 Wrangler II

Winchester Model 55

Winchester Model 94XTR
Similar to the Model 94 Standard except: higher grade wood; checkered stock & forearm; 30-30 or 375 Win.; the 375 has recoil pad; add 25% for 375 Win.
Estimated Value: $180.00 - $225.00

Winchester Model 94XTR Angle Eject
Similar to the Model 94XTR except an "angle eject" feature was added in 1984; in 1986 Winchester called it "side eject;" made in calibers 30-30, 7x30 Waters, 307, 356, or 357 Win.; 7x30 Waters has 7-shot magazine & 24" barrel; other models have 6-shot magazines & 20" barrels; add 10% for 7x30 Waters
Estimated Value: $205.00 - $275.00

Winchester Model 94 Side Eject
Similar to the Model 94 Standard except: "Side Eject" feature; calibers 32 Win. special, 30-30, 308, 356, 375 Win. or 7x30 Waters; 6-shot magazine; recoil pad; add 10% for checkering
Estimated Value: $165.00 - $205.00

Winchester Ranger Lever Action Side Eject
Similar to the Model 94 Standard in 30-30 caliber with 5-shot magazine; smooth wood stock & forearm; walnut finish
Estimated Value: $175.00 - $215.00

Winchester Model 94 Classic Rifle or Carbine
Similar to the Model 94 Standard except: select walnut stock; scroll engraving
Estimated Value: $180.00 - $225.00

Winchester Model 94 Wrangler
Same as the Model 94 Trapper except: large loop-type finger lever; roll-engraved receiver; 32 Special caliber; 5-shot magazine; no angle eject feature
Estimated Value: $175.00 - $220.00

Winchester Model 94 Wrangler II
Similar to the Model 94 Wrangler except: 38-55 caliber; has angle eject feature
Estimated Value: $280.00 - $225.00

Winchester Model 55
Similar to the Model 94 except: 24" nickel steel barrel
Estimated Value: $550.00 - $690.00

Winchester

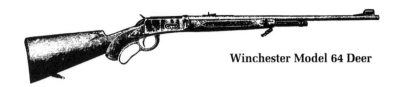

Winchester Model 64 Deer

Winchester Model 94
Wrangler Large Loop Lever
Caliber: 30-30 Win., 44 Rem. magnum (also 44 S&W Special)
Action: Lever action; exposed hammer; repeating; angle-eject; hammer safety; large loop finger lever
Magazine: 5-shot (30-30); 9-shot (44) tubular
Barrel: 16"; round; blued
Stock & Forearm: Smooth walnut straight grip stock and forearm; introduced in 1992; add 6% for 44 Rem. magnum
Estimated Value: $200.00 - $255.00

Winchester Model 64
Similar to the Model 94 & 55 with improvements; 20" or 26" barrel; available in 25-35, 30-30, 32, 219 Zipper (from 1938-41); made from the early 1930's to the late 1950's; add $350.00 for 219 Zipper caliber
Estimated Value: $320.00 - $400.00

Winchester Model 64 Deer
Similar to the Model 64 except: 32 or 30-30 caliber; swivels; checkered pistol grip stock; made from the mid 1930's to mid 1950's
Estimated Value: $400.00 - $500.00

Winchester Model 95

Winchester Model 95 Carbine

Winchester Model 95 Carbine
Similar to the Model 95 except: 22" barrel
Estimated Value: $800.00 - $1,000.00

Winchester Model 1895 Musket
Similar to the Model 95 except: 28" or 30" round nickel steel barrel; full-length forearm; barrel bands; 30-40 gov't caliber; add $300.00 for U.S. Gov't models
Estimated Value: $800.00 - $1,000.00

Winchester Model 95
Caliber: 30-40 Krag, 30-06, 30-30, 303, 35, or 405
Action: Lever action; exposed hammer; repeating
Magazine: 4-shot & 5-shot box
Barrel: 24", 26", 28"; round, octagon, or half octagon
Stock & Forearm: Plain wood straight or pistol grip stock & tapered, lipped forearm; made from about 1895 to the early 1930's; a few thousand early models were built with a flat receiver (add $200.00)
Estimated Value: $720.00 - $900.00

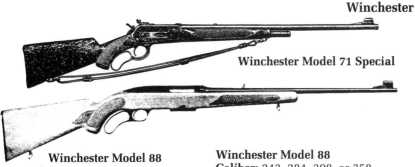

Winchester Model 71 Special

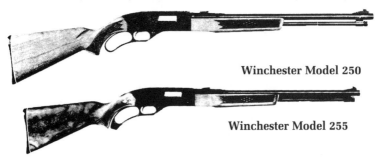

Winchester Model 88

Winchester Model 71
Caliber: 348 Win.
Action: Lever action; exposed hammer; repeating
Magazine: 4-shot tubular
Barrel: 20" or 24"; blued
Stock & Forearm: Plain or checkered walnut pistol grip stock & forearm
Estimated Value: $450.00 - $600.00

Winchester Model 71 Special
Similar to the Model 71 with checkering & swivels
Estimated Value: $520.00 - $650.00

Winchester Model 88
Caliber: 243, 284, 308, or 358
Action: Lever action; hammerless; repeating
Magazine: 4-shot box on late models; 5-shot box on early models; 3-shot box in 284 caliber
Barrel: 22"
Stock & Forearm: Checkered walnut one-piece semi-pistol grip stock & forearm; barrel band
Estimated Value: $295.00 - $370.00

Winchester Model 88 Carbine
Similar to the Model 88 except: plain stock & forearm; 19" barrel
Estimated Value: $315.00 - $395.00

Winchester Model 250

Winchester Model 255

Winchester Model 250
Caliber: 22 short, long, or long rifle
Action: Lever action; hammerless; repeating
Magazine: Tubular; 15 long rifle, 17 longs, or 21 shorts
Barrel: 20½"; blued
Stock & Forearm: Plain or checkered walnut semi-pistol grip stock & forearm
Estimated Value: $110.00 - $135.00

Winchester Model 250 Deluxe
Similar to the Model 250 except: Monte Carlo stock; swivels
Estimated Value: $115.00 - $140.00

Winchester Model 255
Similar to the Model 250 except: 22 magnum caliber; 11-shot magazine
Estimated Value: $120.00 - $150.00

Pocket Guide to Rifles

Winchester

Winchester Model 9422 & 9422 XTR
Caliber: 22 short, long, long rifle, or 22 magnum
Action: Lever action; exposed hammer; repeating
Magazine: Tubular; 15 long rifle, 17 longs, or 21 shorts. 11 - 22 magnum
Barrel: 20"
Stock & Forearm: Plain or checkered wood straight grip stock & forearm; barrel band; 9422XTR has higher grade wood & finish also checkered
Estimated Value: $220.00 - $275.00

Winchester Model 9422
Win-Tuff, Win-Cam
Similar to the Model 9422 except: laminated stock of brown dyed wood (Win-Tuff) or green & brown dyed wood (Win-Cam); add 4% for magnum or Win-Cam.
Estimated Value: $220.00 - $275.00

Winchester Model 9422

Winchester Model 9422XTR Classic Rifle
Similar to the Model 9422XTR except: satin-finish walnut pistol grip stock & forearm; fluted comb & crescent steel buttplate; curved finger lever; longer forearm; 22½" barrel; 22 or 22 magnum caliber
Estimated Value: $200.00 - $250.00

Winchester Model 150
Caliber: 22 short, long, or long rifle
Action: Lever action; hammerless; repeating
Magazine: Tubular; 15 long rifle, 17 longs, or 21 shorts
Barrel: 20½"; blued
Stock & Forearm: Straight grip stock & forearm; barrel band; alloy receiver
Estimated Value: $105.00 - $130.00

Winchester Model 1890

Winchester Model 06

Winchester Model 1890
Caliber: 22 short, long, or long rifle
Action: Slide action; exposed hammer; repeating
Magazine: Tubular; 11 long rifle, 12 longs, or 15 shorts
Barrel: 24"; octagon
Stock & Forearm: Plain wood straight grip stock & grooved slid handle
Estimated Value: $380.00 - $475.00

Winchester Model 06
Caliber: 22 short, long, or long rifle
Action: Slide action; exposed hammer; repeating
Magazine: Tubular; 11 long rifle, 12 longs, or 15 shorts
Barrel: 20"; blued
Stock & Forearm: Plain wood straight or pistol grip stock, grooved or plain slide handle; blued or nickel trimmed receiver
Estimated Value: $340.00 - $425.00

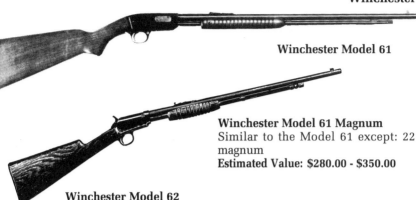

Winchester Model 61

Winchester Model 61 Magnum
Similar to the Model 61 except: 22
magnum
Estimated Value: $280.00 - $350.00

Winchester Model 62

Winchester Model 62 & 62A
Caliber: 22 short, long, or long rifle
Action: Slide action; exposed
hammer; repeating
Magazine: Tubular; 14 long rifle, 16
longs, or 20 shorts
Barrel: 23"; blued
Stock & Forearm: Walnut straight
grip stock & grooved slide handle; it
became 62A in the 1940's with
internal improvements; a gallery
model was available chambered for
22 shot only.
Estimated Value: $310.00 - $390.00

Winchester Model 61
Caliber: 22 short, long, or long rifle
Action: Slide action; repeating
Magazine: Tubular; 14 long rifle, 16
longs, or 20 shorts
Barrel: 24"; blued; round or octagon
Stock & Forearm: Plain wood semi-
pistol grip stock & grooved slide
handle
Estimated Value: $285.00 - $355.00

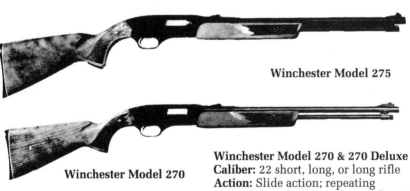

Winchester Model 275

Winchester Model 270

Winchester Model 270 & 270 Deluxe
Caliber: 22 short, long, or long rifle
Action: Slide action; repeating
Magazine: Tubular; 15 long rifle, 17
longs, or 21 shorts
Barrel: 20½"
Stock & Forearm: Walnut or plastic
pistol grip stock & slide handle;
plain or checkered; model 270
Deluxe has Monte Carlo stock
Estimated Value: $85.00 - $120.00

Winchester Model 275 & 275 Deluxe
Similar to the Model 270 & 270
Deluxe except: 22 magnum caliber
Estimated Value: $90.00 - $125.00

Winchester

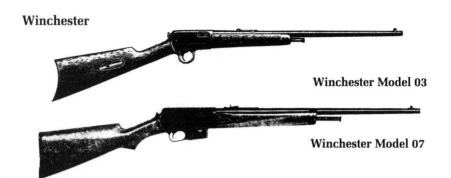

Winchester Model 03

Winchester Model 07

Winchester Model 03
Caliber: 22 short, long, or long rifle
Action: Semi-automatic
Magazine: 10-shot tubular, in stock
Barrel: 20"; blued
Stock & Forearm: Plain or checkered wood semi-pistol grip or straight stock; made from 1903 to the mid 1930's
Estimated Value: $225.00 - $300.00

Winchester Model 05
Similar to the Model 03 except: 32 Win. or 35 Win. caliber; 5 or 10-shot detachable box magazine; 22" barrel; made to about 1920
Estimated Value: $270.00 - $350.00

Winchester Model 07
Caliber: 351
Action: Semi-automatic; hammerless
Magazine: 5 or 10-shot detachable box
Barrel: 20"; blued
Stock & Forearm: plain wood semi-pistol grip stock & forearm; made from 1907 to late 1950's
Estimated Value: $315.00 - $425.00

Winchester Model 10
Similar to the Model 07 except: 401 caliber; 4-shot magazine; made until the mid 1930's.
Estimated Value: $320.00 - $430.00

Winchester Model 63

Winchester Model 74

Winchester Model 74
Caliber: 22 long rifle only or 22 short only
Action: Semi-automatic
Magazine: Tubular; 14 long rifle; 20 shorts; in stock
Barrel: 24"; blued
Stock & Forearm: Plain wood one-piece semi-pistol grip stock & forearm
Estimated Value: $150.00 - $200.00

Winchester Model 63
Caliber: 22 long rifle, high speed; 22 long rifle Super X
Action: Semi-automatic
Magazine: 10-shot tubular, in stock
Barrel: 20" or 23"; blued
Stock & Forearm: Plain wood pistol grip stock & forearm
Estimated Value: $320.00 - $425.00

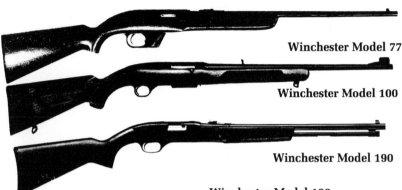

Winchester Model 77

Winchester Model 100

Winchester Model 190

Winchester Model 77
Caliber: 22 long rifle
Action: Semi-automatic
Magazine: 8-shot detachable
Barrel: 22"; blued
Stock & Forearm: Plain walnut one-piece semi-pistol grip stock & forearm
Estimated Value: $105.00 - $135.00

Winchester Model 77 Tubular
Similar to the Model 77 except: 15-shot tubular magazine
Estimated Value: $110.00 - $140.00

Winchester Model 100
Caliber: 243, 284, or 308
Action: Semi-automatic; gas operated
Magazine: 4-shot clip; 10-shot clip in 284
Barrel: 19" or 22"; blued
Stock & Forearm: Checkered walnut one-piece stock & forearm; swivels
Estimated Value: $300.00 - $375.00

Winchester Model 100 Carbine
Similar to the Model 100 except: without checkering; 19" barrel; barrel bands
Estimated Value: $310.00 - $390.00

Winchester Model 190
Caliber: 22 short, long, or long rifle
Action: Semi-automatic; hammerless
Magazine: Tubular; 15 long rifle, 17 longs, or 21 shorts
Barrel: 22"
Stock & Forearm: Plain semi-pistol grip stock & forearm
Estimated Value: $80.00 - $100.00

Winchester Model 190 Carbine
Similar to the Model 190 except: 20½" barrel; barrel band; swivels
Estimated Value: $85.00 - $110.00

Winchester Model 290
Caliber: 22 short, long, or long rifle
Action: Semi-automatic
Magazine: Tubular; 15 long rifle, 17 longs, or 21 shorts
Barrel: 20½"
Stock & Forearm: Checkered walnut pistol grip stock & forearm
Estimated Value: $85.00 - $110.00

Winchester Model 490
Caliber: 22 long rifle
Action: Semi-automatic
Magazine: 5, 10, or 15-shot clip
Barrel: 22"; blued
Stock & Forearm: Checkered walnut one-piece pistol grip stock & forearm
Estimated Value: $130.00 - $165.00

Modern Guns

Revised Ninth Edition

by Russell and Steve Quertermous

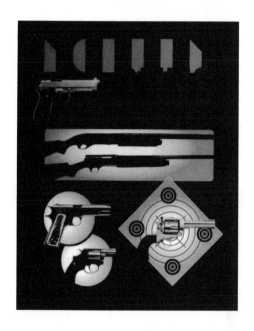

In the 15 years of its existence this book has become a standard reference for gun dealers, hunters, sportsmen and firearms enthusiasts all across the United States. This huge collection features 480 pages crammed full of valuable information and photographs that are indispensable to gun lovers. Over 2,250 models of rifles, handguns and shotguns from 1900 to the present are described and priced in excellent and very good condition with suggested retail prices for those models still in production. More than 1,800 illustrations are included to aid in identification. This popular guide contains model name, gauge or caliber, action, finish on stock and forearm, barrel, cylinder or magazine, sights, weight and length, comments and current market values.

Modern Guns is available from your favorite bookseller. If you are unable to find this book in your area, it's available from Collector Books, P.O. Box 3009, Paducah, KY 42002-3009 at $12.95 plus $2.00 for postage and handling.

8½x11 • 480 Pgs. • PB   **$12.95**

COLLECTOR BOOKS
A division of Schroeder Publishing Co., Inc.

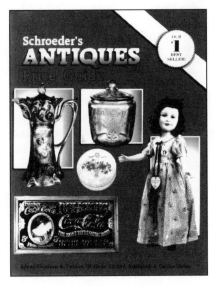